How to Manage in the Public Sector

GORDON CHASE / ELIZABETH C. REVEAL

with contributions to the prologue by

MICHAEL DUKAKIS / RICHARD E. NEUSTADT
GRAHAM T. ALLISON, JR. / MARK H. MOORE

▲ ADDISON-WESLEY PUBLISHING COMPANY
Reading, Massachusetts / Menlo Park, California
London / Amsterdam / Don Mills, Ontario / Sydney

Library of Congress Cataloging in Publication Data

Chase, Gordon.
    How to manage in the public sector.

    1. Public administration   I. Reveal, Elizabeth C.
II. Title.
JF1351.C42   1983   350   82-16406
ISBN 0-201-10127-0

ISBN 0-201-10127-0
ABCDEGHIJ-DO-89876543

Preface

I first met Gordon Chase in the summer of 1979 when I was a participant in the Program for Senior Executives in State and Local Government at Harvard—a program which Gordon chaired and which he had been instrumental in creating.

He was an incredible teacher. His enthusiasm for public service and his belief that government really could work were absolutely contagious. We all thought we knew something about public management; about state and local problems and the difficulty of implementing programs with too few resources and too many demands. But Gordon simply dazzled us; it was like being club tennis champion and having an opportunity to "hit a few" with Bjorn Borg—there was just no comparison.

After Gordon's death in January of 1980, Michael Dukakis, his friend and colleague, accepted the responsibility for finding an author and shepherding the completion of a book that Gordon had been working on for a number of years. Originally its subject was to have been health care services in New York City, but over time the scope and focus of the project changed, becoming a more general discussion of how to get the public's business done, and done well.

I began working on the manuscript in the summer of 1980. This final version comprises material which was to have been the first section of a longer work on all aspects of public agency management: Gordon Chase's answer—for public managers—to Paul Samuelson's *Economics*. It is terribly sad that he is not here to complete the comprehensive work he envisioned.

It is the premise of this book that public management is an art, not a science—and a people art, at that. But, like art, public management *can* be taught and a manager's skills refined. Artists perfect the rudiments of their craft before they go onstage or exhibit in a gallery. Public managers do not always have such luxury, as learning by doing is more often the order of the day. Many campaign workers have become agency heads, and line workers administrators, overnight as a result of political or program circumstances. The purpose of this book is to provide guidance in recognizing and practicing the rudiments of public sector relationships; to help those who are now managers, students hoping to become managers, and others who aspire to public service to understand the environment in which they work. It is intended to help in the fine art of dealing with executives, legislators, reporters, the public, community organizations and overhead staff: the players who are the everyday business of public management.

The text is organized into two main sections: one on the public manager's relationships within government and the other on relationships outside of government. It looks at bosses and chief executives, overhead agencies, other elected officials and legislators, community groups, good-government groups, special interests, and the press. Each chapter describes the nature of the players' powers, their motives and how they operate, how they affect the public manager, and how public managers can and should deal with them. The approach is a personal one, based on Gordon's twenty years of experience at the federal, state, and local levels, and my own experience as a state and local manager. It is an exercise in practical application, not academic research, and I hope it will convey a sense of what it is like to administer programs on the public's behalf.

Obviously no one can solve the problems of implementing government policy without understanding the nature of government and the environment in which these problems must be resolved. The history of government is rife with examples of solutions applied to the wrong problem, in the wrong way, at the wrong time. If this book helps public managers to understand their environment a little better, and politicians, the public, and the press to understand public managers a little better, it will have served its purpose.

Many people have provided help and assistance during the completion of this book. Special thanks go to Mary Kurkjian, a student and later colleague of Gordon's who first suggested my involvement in the project; Michael Dukakis, whose patience as weeks turned into months and whose interest and encouragement were much appreciated; Stuart Johnson, from Addison-Wesley, who tolerated this novice writer well; and especially Dorothy Wilkerson, who is, simply, the best typist I have ever encountered. Very special assistance was provided by Alan Campbell, Nathan Leventhal, Glenn Sparrow, and David Garson, who read earlier drafts and provided many useful suggestions and comments. Allen Kraus, as always, curbed my tendency toward multiple adjectives and provided many useful editorial suggestions.

Thanks also to my intern in the summer of 1980, Saadya Sternberg, who helped to sift through mounds of papers and old drafts; to Chris Chase, Gordon's son, who, while compiling Gordon's class notes and papers for the Kennedy School, uncovered many relevant writings and anecdotes; and to Naomi Chase, Gordon's wife (and talented author and public official in her own right), who has patiently waited for the book's publication. I hope the final product meets with all of their approval.

Elizabeth C. Reveal
New York City
December 1982

Contents

Prologue:
The Legacy of
Gordon Chase

ACCORDING TO MICHAEL DUKAKIS

Those of us who knew Gordon Chase did not have to be told that we were in the presence of an unusual man. Not that Gordon overwhelmed you when you first met him. I remember meeting him initially in 1974 when I was trying to persuade him to take over the trouble-ridden Metropolitan Boston Transit Authority. He was tall but tended to slouch a bit. A fashion plate he wasn't. In fact, I remember asking him once if his olive corduroy suit was the only one he owned, and I don't recall ever getting a straight answer.

It was the Gordon Chase in action who bowled people over. Whether in the classroom or in government, he was something. He had an extraordinary ability to inspire others. He cared deeply about people, all people, whether they were his students, the people who worked for him, or the people he tried to serve and help in the community at large.

He was also a bundle of contradictions. He was an ex-Marine and a political liberal. Spit and polish simply didn't apply to his personal appearance—the sweater with the holes in its sleeves, the corduroy suit—but when it came to maintaining standards, he was very tough indeed; and those to which he held himself were the most exacting of all. He loved good conversation, but he managed his time very, very carefully. He could have taught without a note, but I never saw him before a class without elaborate notes that he had written and rewritten and which he would be reviewing right up to the moment when his class was scheduled to begin. He was not a scholar in the traditional sense of the word, but he had an ability, rare in a manager, to step back from what he was doing; to reflect; and, as this book so eloquently demonstrates, to write about the job of a public manager in a unique and extraordinary way.

He also had the ability to laugh at his own foibles and weaknesses. Some of his best moments in the classroom involved his description of how he had goofed, particularly in trying to handle the New York City press. And his students loved him for it, for who in government has not made a hash of relations with the press at some time in his or her career?

I never had the opportunity to work for him, and we worked together in state government for only a few short weeks. But all who ever worked for him have told me the same thing—that he was the best boss they ever had. He touched them; lifted their sights; inspired them to do more than they ever thought possible. *Nothing* was impossible, so far as Gordon was concerned. If New York City had never been able to test more than ten thousand a year for lead poisoning, Gordon would suggest one hundred thousand or two hundred thousand. His staff would be incredulous. The man must be crazy; how can we possibly do it?

But they did it. Hard work; reaching out to the community; the skillful use of the media; the simple discovery that mothers who were informed of the danger of lead paint were the most effective people to protect their children—by such means those previously impossible goals were met and in many cases exceeded. Gordon was also a great believer in building competition into his programs and agencies. He'd bet one of his managers a dinner at "21" that he couldn't make a certain target, and the manager would make it if only to get that meal out of Gordon. He challenged private hospitals in New York City to participate in his methadone maintenance program, and their desire to "do better" than his own publicly sponsored clinics stimulated a far greater commitment to drug treatment than those hospitals had ever displayed before.

Of course, one of Gordon's greatest assets as a public manager was his own ability to get things done in an often difficult and complicated political environment. He pushed himself hard. He worked long hours. He believed deeply in the capacity of government to change things for the better—and his own achievements were proof enough that the job could be done.

He was extraordinarily versatile. He began his government career as a foreign service officer. Then he went to the White House, although still in foreign and national security affairs. But he left foreign policy to become executive director of the Equal Employment Opportunity Commission. It was only after both his foreign affairs service and his civil rights work that he moved into the field of human services, and then first as a manager, not a maker and shaper of policy.

But Gordon's greatest strength as a public manager was his understanding of the complicated political environment within which a public manager has to operate and the importance of mastering that environment. No dry-as-dust public administration textbook discussions of the differences between staff and line agencies for him. In fact, if there was one thing he avoided like the plague, it was the tendency exhibited by many other public managers to spend months of their time on structural reorganizations instead of program delivery.

The political environment that too often stopped managers in their tracks was, for Gordon, the real thing. What kind of mayor, governor, or president are you working for? How do you handle chiefs and their staffs? What about the "overhead" agencies—budget, personnel, general services? Advocacy groups and community activists? The political "talkers"? How do you get your personnel requests through the budget bureau? What do you do when four hundred community activists blockade the entrance to your office? How do you deal with the press and make them an ally, not an adversary?

It all seems so obvious now. But at the time that Gordon began this book, there was virtually nothing written on the subject for public managers, and there were very few people in schools of public administration and management teaching about it.

And how Gordon Chase could teach! I remember the first Program for Senior Executives in State and Local Government at the John F. Kennedy School of Government in the summer of 1979. Gordon and I were the chairman and vice-chairman respectively of the new program, and we had some forty tough, seasoned senior managers in the program from twenty states across the country. This is what they had to say about Gordon at the end of a bruising three weeks:

"Sensitive," said one.

"A master," said another.

"Outstanding," said still another.

And perhaps the most perceptive comment of all: "The best . . . he has succeeded and failed."

For Gordon could admit failure as well as relish his

successes—and he could talk about his failures in class not only with great good humor but in a way that made them important lessons for his students. "Gordon's bromides," they called them, as they pleaded with him to spend just one more hour in class with them before they headed for home.

Yes, he was a great teacher. But in the end his greatest love was in managing, in doing, in helping to make the world a better place. He had, in Graham Allison's words, "an enormous enthusiasm for the tasks of government." He believed that people, acting through the instrumentality of government, could reach for the stars; solve problems; make life better for us all.

I'll never forget the morning he came into my office in the summer of 1979 after he had received a call from the new secretary of the then U.S. Department of Health, Education and Welfare asking if he might go down to Washington to talk with her about the undersecretary's job in the agency.

"Gordon," I said, "you're up to your ears in our executive program. Brandeis is about to give you tenure. How can you possibly think about picking up and heading for HEW?"

And there he sat, like a little boy in a candy store— eyes positively glistening—saying over and over again: "But Mike, this is it. This is where it's at. It's my profession. *It's where you can really make a difference.*"

This book is his legacy. This is Gordon as he spoke, as he worked, as he taught.

It is a very different look at the world of government and of public management. It is, in my view, a breakthrough in texts of this kind. For it talks about the job of public manager as it is in the real world of politicians, reporters, advocates, and bureaucrats. It should be required reading for anyone who is trying to manage programs and people in government. It should also be required reading for those outside of government who seek a real understanding of what managing effectively in the public sector is all about.

ACCORDING TO RICHARD E. NEUSTADT

I first met Gordon Chase at the doorway of the situation room in the basement of the west wing of the White House. The situation room was then a new facility; Gordon Chase was helping to get it into shape. McGeorge Bundy, White House assistant for National Security Affairs, had spotted Gordon at our London embassy, where he was doing a remarkable administrative job, and by some means or other had got him detailed to the National Security Council staff, Bundy's own. As an occasional consultant I had heard of Chase but had not met him when I almost collided with him in that doorway. He was coming out; I was going in. We stopped, introduced ourselves and chatted for a moment, then went our ways.

He, I daresay, soon forgot our encounter; I did not. I was so startled by it, drawn up so short, that it remains a vivid memory even after twenty years. For in that moment I had felt the force of an extraordinary personality. Gordon seemed at once alert, contained, warm, serious, and funny, all reflected in his intelligent and mobile face. I found the combination both attractive and arresting and resolved to keep an eye on him.

That I failed to do, to my regret, although I did keep track of him. The next time we actually met was almost a decade later in New York. Chase had left the foreign service and the White House staff, to the dismay of all, as I was told; had done a much praised piece of work in the entirely different setting of the Equal Employment Opportunity Commission; and now was flourishing, by all accounts, as New York City's Health Services Administrator. He was managing the doctors without being one himself, a feat that was greatly admired and one that was very reassuring to the mayor, John Lindsay, who had taken a chance—and an imaginative leap—in giving Chase the job. My purpose when we met was to subvert the mayor by urging Gordon to give thought to a still different sort of job, teaching what had been his field, entrepreneurship in the public sector—or, more broadly, public management.

My colleagues and I had been led to Chase because he had a reputation for being, among managers, unusually analytical—able to stand outside himself and watch what he was doing—and at the same time being, among Lindsay's aides, possessed of unusual ego-control, rumored indeed to have a sense of humor even (and not least) about himself. It was all true, as we were to find out; but Gordon was at first reluctant to consider teaching. It seemed to him a passive occupation: challenging, perhaps, but not on the same order as a fresh administrative task. I told him he could find it more so, and indeed I think that is the reason he eventually agreed to come to us and try. A challenge was a thing Gordon Chase could not resist.

He did come, did try, found the challenge grueling; found the effort to meet student needs, to feed their curiosity, enhance their understanding, build their skills, the toughest work he'd done—or so he told me— but eminently stimulating, satisfying to him. Characteristically he threw himself into it. He was a rare practitioner in his capacity—which grew with his hard work—to move all the way from brilliant management to effective teaching, thinking about how to teach along with the subject matter and ultimately making the effort to ensure that his thoughts were accessible and useful to the rest of us. When he died—in a particularly senseless automobile accident—he left a host of deeply affected students at two universities, a double set of colleagues who have found him irreplaceable, and the manuscript of what is now this book. In the best sense it is a how-to-do-it book, and from it one can glean how Gordon did it—with the qualities I glimpsed on his face there in that White House doorway.

ACCORDING TO GRAHAM T. ALLISON, JR. AND MARK H. MOORE

Our colleagues, Dick Neustadt and Mike Dukakis, have written eloquently about Gordon Chase's presence— his idealism, his determination, his imagination, the sheer force of character that inspired people around him. No one who knew Gordon could remain untouched by his character. Not to put too fine a point on it, in our eyes he was a hero. Left to our own devices, then, we too would eulogize him in these terms.

But we have a different assignment. Our job is to size up the intellectual product he has left behind, and to assess the process that yielded this book as a strategy for learning about effective public management. In the end, this cannot be separated from Gordon Chase as an individual since it is *his* practical wisdom and experience that is contained in this book. It was his unique determination and self-consciousness that allowed a book to be produced from his wide experience. It is his spirit and character that leap from these pages to carry much of the burden of teaching people what effective management is all about. Still, with some effort, we can take a slightly detached view of the book and consider how it fits into the "literature" about public management.

The crucial thing to understand about it is that it is a

how-to book. It is designed to speak to practicing public executives about the nature of their jobs, and to offer ideas about tools and techniques that a successful public manager has found to be helpful to him. An academic social scientist reviewing the book could find much to criticize. How general is the characterization of the public manager's job? The responsibilities and tasks of government officials may change with changes in the tasks and institutional arrangements of government. Perhaps the conception of the job presented here was appropriate for a brief historical period, but is now becoming outmoded as the public sector shrinks, as financing becomes more restrictive, as the pursuit of "representativeness" yields (temporarily) to the pursuit of "politically neutral competence," and as public agencies increasingly rely on private sector production to achieve their goals. Similarly, *How to Manage in the Public Sector* may be appropriate for state and local managers of human services, but is it equally appropriate for managers engaged in other tasks at other levels of government, and in different positions within organizations? On these questions, the book is mostly silent. Certainly no evidence is presented about the current distribution of public sector jobs or about the institutional trends that are affecting the character of those jobs. Finally, the book's prescriptions about how to manage certain aspects of the job may appear to be mere assertions. True, they may be supported by Chase's successful experience. But as propositions they are supported neither by a convincing deductive logic nor by a systematically gathered body of empirical evidence. As a result, their status as valuable prescriptions could well be in doubt.

In our view, such academic criticisms miss much of the point of Chase's work because they fail to understand the content of professional knowledge (as distinct from scientific knowledge) and the character of professional training. In the academic's view, professional knowledge should consist of a set of propositions about the world that are known to be true and are relevant to the professional tasks. Professional training should consist of teaching these propositions. Thus, professional training in medicine should depend heavily on knowledge of biology and biochemistry; professional training in the law must depend heavily on mastering the complex logical structure that incorporates hundreds of particular cases into a coherent body of substantive law; professional training in architecture must depend on knowledge of propositions drawn from physics, engineering, sociology, and aesthetics.

But simply to state this view is to reveal the difficulties. The problem is partly one of the sufficiency of scientific knowledge. At any given moment, the number of propositions known to be true is insufficient to the solution of problems facing practitioners. Equally important but more subtle is the fact that practical problem solving always involves more than empirical knowledge of relationships in the world. It also involves the definition of purposes (which has normative content) and the conception of possible solutions (which depend on imagination). Finally, professional practice often involves solving particular problems which present themselves, with unique possibilities to be exploited and unique difficulties to be avoided. Part of being a successful practitioner is giving due regard to what is unusual in a situation as well as to what is general.

These observations lead us to the conclusion that professional knowledge is something different from a set of well-established propositions, and that professional training is something different from mastering a given set of propositions. Professional knowledge must include contingent ideas that, in some sense, serve in place of better-developed propositions until they are developed, but in another sense may always be contingent because they can and should be modified in particular situations. In addition, professional knowledge must include some definition of the common problems faced by the profession, and some conception of what actions the profession can take to solve particular problems. Professional knowledge is, above all, a way of thinking about the problems one faces rather than a clever set of answers. Professional training involves engaging students in acquiring knowledge. But, in addition, it must go beyond knowledge to build a commitment to the profession and to create a profound sense of the responsibilities and virtues of the profession.

In these terms, Chase and Reveal's book is a major contribution. It establishes a conception of the tasks of public managers that—perhaps surprisingly—emphasizes the political dimensions of the public manager's job. The daily struggle to maintain a mandate, a position, and sufficient control over management tools such as budgeting and personnel that it becomes possible for the public manager to achieve his (or her) objectives is central in the focus of this book, as it is the operating experience of most public executives. The fact that this task figures so prominently in the experience of a public executive like Chase, who was naturally inclined more to the organization of production than to the tasks of political authorization, signals an important lesson for those who would learn and teach public management. The management of a public official's "external" political environment is as fundamental to the success of a manager as is the ability to organize and motivate production among subordinates. Beyond establishing "political management" as a central task of "nonpolitical administration," *How to Manage in the Public Sector* is full of useful advice about how to diagnose a situation and discern what actions are possible, and provides some rough sense of what is generally successful. Thus it is a major contribution to the development of professional knowledge about public management, and useful to those who must teach people who aspire to major positions of public responsibility. Chase is not Chester Barnard. But he has taken a large step in that direction.

To the extent that our judgment of this volume is accurate, its production reveals both the virtues and the difficulties of trying to build professional knowledge and training from the practical wisdom and experience of public sector officials. This book is powerful precisely because it does so much more than convey a set of propositions: it expresses the virtues, the tasks, the modes of thinking, and the clearer solutions that characterize outstanding professional practice in the area of public management. In our view, it is not possible to do this without the benefit of broad and deep professional experience. At the same time, however, there is much here that can be improved. Propositions can be refined and tested. Curiosities about the generality of Chase and Reveal's views can profitably be pursued. We hope that such intellectual enterprise is unleashed.

Finally, it is important to remember that this was the product of a truly unusual man. He was unusual in two respects: as a practitioner with an extraordinary record and— most miraculously of all—as a practitioner who could subject himself to the intellectual discipline of producing a book of general value to his professional constituency. We hope that his courage, his determination, and his insight will be replicated. But our keen sense of the rarity of these qualities makes us mourn his untimely death deeply. Our professional community has lost a leading light. For that reason, we are all the more grateful for this intellectual legacy as well as his professional attainments.

1/ Managers, Players, and Problems

WHO ARE THE MANAGERS?

Implementation—the process by which government policy is turned into practice—is, ultimately, what government is all about. Policy makers decide what *should* be done, but citizens experience what *is* done.

What matters to people on the receiving end of government services is not legislative intent or political rhetoric but what happens. Is the garbage picked up? Do the police respond quickly to an emergency? Do the buses show up on time? Are there qualified teachers and firefighters and welfare workers? That the answer to these questions is so often no suggests that implementation—actually operating government programs—is as difficult as it important.

In the end, elected public officials are held accountable for government's performance. But it is nonelected officials—public managers—who really determine that performance; who have day-to-day responsibility for operating programs, responding to emergencies, and accounting for the dollars, employees, clients, paper, machines, and facilities that are the government's business.

Typically, agency heads, commissioners, cabinet members, and people of similar rank are considered "public managers." We read about them, we see them on television, and we associate them with the agencies they run and the services they provide. But public managers are of more humble rank as well; in fact, a public manager is anyone who has responsibility for spending public monies and directing public employees toward ends authorized by chief executives and legislatures or mandated by courts.

Public managers can be police chiefs or insurance commissioners, school principals or hospital administrators, welfare supervisors or prison wardens; or any of the thousands of other public servants responsible for everything from water to roads, mental health to education. Collectively these managers supervise billions of dollars of public resources and hundreds of thousands of employees. In more than seventy thousand towns, cities, counties, and states—in addition to the federal government—it is the public manager, more than anyone else, who is responsible for what actually happens when government, in countless ways, involves itself with the lives of its citizens.

Yet with their enormous responsibility and influence, public managers are little understood and much maligned. The public often characterizes these officials as hapless bureaucrats whose interest in the quality of services goes about as far as their monthly paycheck. Elected officials assume that these appointed colleagues will turn rhetoric into operation with a minimum of resources and a maximum of success. Pressure groups and special interests assume that public managers can, and should, accede to their demands and priorities. And the press—ah yes, the media—expect these officials to aspire to sainthood and to willingly and cheerfully accept continual public scrutiny.

Public managers have a different perspective on the problems of government than do elected officials or citizens using services. Their objective is not to win reelection, although their careers often depend on the political fortunes of those who select them for office. They know what services they are supposed to be providing, and to whom, but they cannot be "on the spot" for every telephone conversation or interaction between their employees and the public.

This chapter and those which follow examine the world of government from the perspective of the public manager. While the observations and comments are made, as often as not, through the eyes of the agency head, they apply to mid-level managers and other government professionals as well. Certainly agency heads deal with their peers in the environment more often than with their peers' subordinates. But mid-managers have counterparts in other agencies, other levels of government, and other groups and institutions; and mid-managers' jobs, and the nature of the environment in which they must work, are more like an agency head's than they are different.

Not all managers experience the same degree of interaction with legislators, overhead staff, other elected officials, community groups, or the press; but all are at risk of being exposed to these competing, and sometimes conflicting, interests.

What makes public management so hard—and so interesting— is that all these players act simultaneously, with few clear lines of authority, constantly changing public mandates, and frequent turnover of people. Getting the garbage picked up, a child treated for lead poisoning, a subway to the station on time, or an elderly person a Social Security check may not seem herculean tasks. But when they are multiplied hundreds of times over, and their execution occurs in the context of the manager's environment, the real challenge of government becomes clear. The tasks can be done, and done well, by public managers who master this world; but such tasks can easily elude managers who are befuddled by the politics around them, disconcerted by the mixed signals they hear, and unsure of their own agenda and purpose.

Managers operate in a highly political and complex environment. Managers who produce are managers who have learned to turn internal and external relationships to their advantage; who know how to anticipate conflict, promote their agenda, and earn the professional respect of varied and diverse associates. Failure comes often to managers who have not mastered this environment, or taken its pitfalls and perils seriously. To understand this environment requires an appreciation of who the players are and why they are important.

WHO ARE THE PLAYERS?

One of the key dimensions of a public manager's job is dealing with the other players on the scene, whose help, cooperation, and support are always important, and sometimes crucial. These are players whom the manager does not control, and who have their own independent interests and agendas.

These "other players" generally fall into three categories:

- those in the manager's immediate executive circle—the chief executive or boss, other agency heads, and subordinates.
- those outside of the immediate executive circle, but

still within government—officials at other levels of government, legislators and judges, and persons elected to such local and state offices as attorney general, comptroller, and secretary of state.

• those players outside of government—the special interests, community advocates, good-government groups, professional associations, and the media.

Other players can affect the manager in a number of welcome and not so welcome ways. They can provide or withhold necessary clearances, authorizations, and approvals—on budget, personnel, procurement, or regulation—that determine whether programs will flourish or wither. They can provide political support, or they can turn political power against a manager's agency and program. And they can cooperate actively and participate in a program's management and operation—through volunteer services, donation of time and skills—or organize grass roots opposition to a manager's goals and strategies. Determining who is likely to do what, to whom, and when is a skill as well as a talent.

WHY DOES IT MATTER?

For agency heads and other public managers, the business of dealing with the players in the environment is at once critical and unavoidable. But, as a group, public managers do not seem particularly good at it.

Papers, magazines, news shows, case studies, and textbooks are filled with examples of managers who fail to play their environment skillfully. As a matter of fact, there seem to be far more agency heads who fail miserably with one or another player than there are managers with well-earned reputations for handling other players successfully. This is true in part because it is difficult to appease a wide variety of interests and still make the tough decisions required to operate public programs. It is due partly to managers' tendencies to specialize—to be "great on the hill" or "tight with the mayor" or a special interest's "man in the statehouse"—failing to realize that it is important to deal skillfully with all the players, not just one or two.

Finally, it is true because all managers face situations where they must align themselves with one player at the expense of another in order to initiate and maintain their programs. On such occasions the manager needs "money in the bank"—stored up goodwill from a track record of professionalism, fairness, and success to ensure that alienated players will come back to the fold, and that others will not shy from trusting the manager in the future.

In sum, the business of dealing with the players on the scene is not only important and unavoidable—it is tough. What follows is an exploration of the characteristics of each of the categories of players and some observations and battle-tested methods for improving the chances for success.

2 / Managers, Bosses, and Chiefs

One of the things I had to figure out very quickly when I became Health Services Administrator was how I was going to deal with City Hall. My credit there was very important to me. That was where I'd got my job and that was where I was going to keep it. Moreover, I knew enough about New York by then to know that I would need their help.

An administrator in New York City who has City Hall one hundred percent behind him has at least a chance of getting something done. Without that support, he doesn't have a prayer. The overhead agencies alone would eat you alive—to say nothing of the vested community interests in town. When a big contributor called the mayor and complained about what I was doing, I wanted the mayor to hear my side of it and, if I was right on the merits, to call up the contributor and tell him he was off base.

That was what I wanted, and my strategy for getting it was fairly straightforward.

Of all the public manager's working relationships, it is the relationship with the boss—the chief executive if you are an agency head, the commissioner or department head if you are a division manager or program director—which is the most important one in the environment. This is the person who appoints and, all too often, fires the manager as well. The chief or boss is the person whose support, or lack of it, will over and over again determine the success or failure of a manager's undertakings. Of all the manager's working relationships, this is the one that demands the greatest attention; if it fails, it matters little what else is done right: the manager is out of a job.

Public managers who work for elected bosses—for mayors, county executives, governors, or presidents—face special problems in coping with their chiefs. This chapter looks primarily at elected chief executives and those aspects of working for an elected chief that demand the manager's attention and care. However, much of the advice pertains also to a program director's or deputy's relationship with the agency head or to managers who find themselves working for other types of elected and appointed officials.

We look first at the nature of elected chiefs and the problems posed for the manager by the chief's characteristics, and then at suggestions for coping with manager / boss relationships, especially when one party has clear political interests and motives.

CHIEF POLITICAL EXECUTIVES: WHAT KIND OF CREATURES ARE THEY?

Understanding the complex relationship between public managers and their chiefs begins with an understanding of the differences between them.

Personalities

First and foremost, the chief is elected and the manager appointed. The chief has no superior and is accountable only to the electorate, the voters who put the chief in office, who can grant or deny that office the next time around. As for public managers, they have a constituency of one—the elected chief (or boss) who appointed them.

Public managers would do well to remember that chief executives are, by definition, successful politicians. This success implies personality characteristics important to a manager's life. The chief has campaigned long and hard in a very rough game indeed and, regardless of outward appearance, is likely to be savvy, tough, energetic, and hard driving. The chief is likely to value these characteristics in public managers—as long as the managers don't employ them to compete with the chief.

To withstand the pounding from opponents, critics, and the press which any chief executive must expect, the chief is also likely to have a sizable ego. People with large egos believe they are good and like to hear from others that they are. Public managers who speak well of their bosses out of earshot (as well as in) won't suffer for the effort. If it is true that you cannot tell a person too many times that he or she is competent, it goes double or triple for chief executives.

Big egos imply a touch of arrogance, a not surprising trait in many chief executives who have worked their way to the top and suddenly find themselves responsible for millions of dollars and thousands of employees, to say nothing of being among the most visible and recognized citizens of their community. Arrogance, or at least strong self-confidence, usually means that the chief is awfully hard to push around. Trying to bluster your way to a chief's respect is unlikely to work for long. What a manager *delivers* is much more significant than what a manager *promises*, and few if any chiefs are too naïve to appreciate the difference.

Chiefs are also, rightly or wrongly, likely to feel that their predecessor in office did a poor job, especially if the campaign was based on attacking the performance of the incumbent. Public managers who do little to distinguish the work of their administration from that of the prior administration are not likely to be favorites in the chief's office.

Most chiefs are beleaguered by media, political rivals and the public. As a result, most of them prize loyalty in their subordinates to a high degree. Politics is more often than not the business of rewarding friends and ignoring (or punishing) enemies. Public managers are by no means immune from being enemies or suffering the consequences of disloyalty.

While the egos and arrogance of chief executives often mellow during their tenure in office, their personality traits will always affect their relationships with staff, agency heads, and consultants. Learning to assess these characteristics and turn them to the manager's advantage is a critical part of public management.

Powers

The exact nature of the relationship between a public manager and a chief executive will vary from case to case depending on the scope of the chief's statutory powers—with respect to legislation, budget, personnel, regulations, and administration. It will vary as well according to the nature of the chief's political power and the chief's philosophy about the role of government. In addition, it will depend on the extent of the chief's prior management experience and personal management style. Manager / chief relationships will also depend on the nature of the manager's agency and its priority personally, politically, or practically for the chief.

PRACTICAL AUTHORITY The principal statutory powers of a chief executive relate to the introduction and approval, or veto, of legislation; the preparation, submission, and administration of the budget; personnel and staffing decisions; and statutory responsibilities for delivery of essential services and for execution of related program and regulatory powers. Executive powers vary greatly by level of government as well as by locality.

With legislation, executive powers vary according to how and when legislation can be introduced, the degree of review and amendment authority the legislature has, and the extent of the chief's veto power. A governor without line-item veto power over legislative budget actions, for example, has considerably less flexibility (and can be less help to the manager trying to block onerous provisions) than one with more detailed veto authority.

The extent to which the chief controls appointments is significant for the manager. Being appointed at the sole discretion of the chief—without statutory tenure, or advice and consent of a legislative body—is considerably different from appointment to a job with fixed tenure, legislative review, and removal only for cause. The manager's appointive status will greatly influence the manager's perception of the chief and the importance of the manager's relationship to the chief.

Chief political executives' powers vary in other areas as well. The procurement or contracting authority of the executive branch is often circumscribed by requirements for legislative or other approval. Often, important executive activities are beyond the direct control of the chief and are handled by independent public corporations or independently elected boards and commissions. School boards, transportation authorities, and health and hospital corporations are typical examples. In these instances the importance of the public manager's relationship with the chief executive will vary directly with the degree of authority the executive has over the manager's agency.

A careful assessment of the scope of the chief's statutory powers is an important prerequisite for any public manager.

POLITICAL AUTHORITY Of equal and sometimes greater importance to the manager is the scope of the chief's political authority. As a general proposition the chief's public support is likely to be greatest at the beginning of the term. Two years after the election, the public manager is much more inclined to want the chief out in front on a controversial issue if the chief's popularity is at eighty-two percent rather than twenty-eight percent.

Public popularity, however, is by no means the sole or even the best measure of the chief's political power. The chief's power within the party is often crucial to his or her ability to influence the legislature, gain cooperation from other elected executive branch officials, and control relationships with "foreign powers"—the judiciary and other levels of government. Presidents and governors generally have substantial influence with their legislatures. Mayors and county executives may be influential with their local councils but less so with their statehouses and with the Congress, with their power usually proportionate to the size of their local delegations to these bodies. Public managers must find ways to evaluate the nature of their chief's political power and determine how and under what circumstances it can be tapped to further agency goals.

PHILOSOPHY The chief executive's personal philosophy of government will influence both the chief's expectations of public managers and when, how, and to what ends the chief is willing to exercise statutory and political clout. Activist chief executives are likely to push these powers to the limit and to demand creative and interventionist programs from their managers. Moderates are more likely to be cautious in the exercise of their powers. Chiefs who believe that government should do and say as little as possible are unlikely to stretch executive prerogatives or twist political arms for a manager's new program or project. While most chiefs enter the job with the expectation of accomplishing something, they will vary greatly on just how dramatic and far-reaching that "something" is going to be. "How active does my chief want this administration to be?" is a question of degree which public managers would do well to ponder before presenting a plan of action to their boss.

Chiefs versus managers

For public managers the most important fact about their elected chief is likely to be that the chief has had little or no prior management experience. In these cases public managers cannot expect from their chiefs the kind of understanding of the manager's problems that grows out of personal experience.

It is remarkable how few elected chiefs have had prior experience in the role. They do not normally climb a career ladder from mayor to governor to president; and they have never, at least to date, gone in the reverse! Among the six presidents taking office from

1960 to 1980, only Carter and Reagan had prior experience as chief executives, as governors respectively for one and two terms of Georgia and California. Previous executive experience is similarly rare among governors and mayors. This is not to say that being a chief elected official is, or should be, a prerequisite to the mayor's or governor's or president's suite. The point is, rather, that the lack of management experience so typical of newly elected chiefs places special burdens on public managers.

Of course, most chiefs have held prior elective office, most commonly in the legislature or in symbolic state or local positions (secretary of state, lieutenant governor, and the like). They bring to the job the sense that governing means making policy, taking positions, and being a "leader," which is all that their previous positions required. They are often unprepared to move from talking to doing—commanding large numbers of people and vast sums of public money—which is what public management is all about.

Why such a large percentage of elected chief executives come to office without administrative experience is beyond the scope of this book. One relevant fact, however, is that it is difficult to make a popular record in public management. A legislator's record is measured easily by the press, since it consists primarily of voting record and legislative portfolio. It is also easy to gain fame as an investigative official—attorney general or chair of a legislative committee—because public corruption is always good copy. Policy making is easy to report. It is a clearly defined event: a vote or a politician's proclamation that this is what government is going to do or should do. The information is all there in a press release or a legislative record. It is an indoor sport.

By contrast, public management—implementation—is not an event at all but a gradual process that starts with a vote and ends, if at all, when a program closes. There is no particular day on which the press, the chief, the legislature, or anyone else can say that a program is or is not working, if indeed anyone—including the public manager—can figure out an answer at all. In some areas, notably human services, it takes a lot of digging even to hazard an educated guess about whether or not a program is being implemented successfully. For all these reasons it is difficult for anyone—especially the press—to assess an official's record as a *manager*.

FIRST TERMS AND NEW BOSSES   Public managers who have been with their chief for more than one term—perhaps for years—have developed their own views of the chief's management ability and style. Typically, however, given the limited tenure of both chiefs and managers, the public manager finds himself or herself working for a new chief—often an inexperienced one.

From the point of view of the public manager, two types of newly elected chiefs are typically encountered: the generals and the policy makers.

The "generals" know that the job has to do with running government, and that management is involved somehow with getting programs going and making things work. But this chief does not really understand the process of implementation. The general sees management as a rather simple military exercise where the general tells the subordinates and the subordinates tell the troops until something finally gets done. This chief sees the problem as one of being demanding and tough; of giving enough orders that everyone gets the message and performs. These qualities may be admirable, but they are hardly sufficient to make government work.

While the general's style may work in the military

(and it sometimes fails there), it certainly does not work well in the civilian part of the public sector. In the military the commander controls all or most of the resources needed to complete the task at hand. But in the public sector the chief rarely if ever has such unilateral control. In addition, the resources public managers *do* control are usually circumscribed by civil service rules, union agreements, and revenue levels. Furthermore, chief elected officials have no brig for the discipline of unruly or disloyal subordinates.

The general does not realize that, in government, implementation is very tough. It is one thing to decide that prison overcrowding must end but quite another to make it happen. Nothing is more disheartening to a public manager than to deliver a particularly tough program or project in one year, only to have the chief resentful because it was not done in six months. Or worse still to have a chief announce at the outset that something will take six months when it cannot possibly be done in less than a year. Educating the "generals" about the realities of public management is an especially frustrating task for managers.

The second type of novice chief is the policy maker. For the policy maker, implementation and management are simply not considered an important part of the chief's responsibility. This chief does not really understand that he or she runs a complex organization, with money, people, and facilities which must be made to perform effectively. Policy makers typically come from legislative backgrounds—they see the job of chief as doing what they did before, only in a bigger way. The policy maker hold this view for a number of reasons: because it is more comfortable, because management may seem boring, because the chief does not really believe that anything can be done in the public sector anyway, or because the chief simply knows no better.

BAD HABITS   While there will obviously be exceptions, some generalizations can be made about newly
elected chiefs—whether they are generals or policy
makers or something in between. New chiefs typically
make several common mistakes (experienced chiefs and
managers may make the same mistakes, but they usually do so out of political or institutional expediency, not
inexperience).

First, a new chief is likely to use time poorly. It takes a
while to get used to the routine of governing and to learn
how to judge the importance of competing demands.
New chiefs have a tendency to spend an enormous
amount of time juggling crises, dealing with the media,
attending ceremonial events, and "making policy."
With rare exceptions do they spend much time managing day-to-day affairs of government—systematically
meeting with their line officers, setting specific goals,
monitoring and evaluating managerial performance,
understanding agency heads' problems and using their
power to break bottlenecks, and doing the multitude of
other things that chiefs can do to make government
more effective.

A second common mistake has to do, not surprisingly,
with people. A chief inexperienced in management and
implementation is likely to make poor judgments about
the kinds of people and skills needed to get the job done.
The new chief may compound his or her own management weaknesses by hiring even less experienced
people for key posts. They in turn take a page from their
boss's book and spend their time politicking, breaking
ground, and taking "courageous" positions. Again,
maybe admirable, but not sufficient. Sometimes the
chief must use the appointment process to satisfy a constituency, sometimes to settle political debts. In either
case performance is not the primary criterion for appointment, in some cases not a criterion at all. In short,

a chief without management experience tends to think—at least at the outset of the administration—that managing is relatively easy and that any bright person can do it. The chief will not reject cabinet nominees *because* they have management experience but will weigh other considerations more heavily.

Sooner or later chiefs began to realize the importance of good management. They start to see that, while all agency heads have trouble implementing policy and operating programs, some consistently deliver and others do not. Over time it becomes clear that managers who can deliver are a help to the chief, while those who cannot are a liability. When the translation is made in terms the chief can understand—power, press, and the purse—management ability suddenly becomes very important indeed.

It is in this context that I viewed John Lindsay, the 103rd mayor of New York City, from 1966 to 1974, and my boss for almost five years. For me he was by far the most important piece of the New York City landscape. No voters had given me my job. No pressure group lobbied for it. My constituency of one was John V. Lindsay. He was City Hall, and that's where the power was, so far as I was concerned. And John Lindsay had power. He was the mayor of New York, and in New York the mayor has power. This is not the case in every big city in the United States. In some cities, for example, mayors have to clear many appointments with legislatures and have relatively little control over their budgets. But not in New York City.

Like many other chief political executives, John Lindsay had had no prior experience in running anything, let alone the second biggest government in the United States with its roughly 350,000 employees and $10 billion budget.* He had been a congressman for years and before that a private lawyer and a staff aide to former attorney general Herbert Brownell.

In effect, Lindsay came from the ranks of the "talkers," and his first four years in office showed it. He made many mistakes; among them, in my view, was his choice of cabinet people. In a number of key positions, he picked "names"—people who were known for their individual work and writings in substantive fields, but not for any particular managerial competence or expertise. Even though some of them turned out to have political skills as well as substantive expertise, Lindsay got burned. Typically, the agency head would say it would be wise that this or that program be delivered, he would get the mayor excited about it, and then he would not be able to deliver. This happened often enough that by his third year in office, Lindsay had learned a couple of things. For one, he had learned that implementation was important. For another, he had learned that it was very hard indeed. He didn't understand exactly what it took to deliver a program, but he appreciated the art and knew that there was more to it than the captain telling the lieutenant, the lieutenant telling the sergeant, and the sergeant telling the troops. Finally, he had learned to tell the difference between someone who delivered and someone who didn't. Of course this is not always easy, since people who don't deliver never come right out and say so. They either

---

*These were the appropriate figures in the late sixties and early seventies. Today New York City has approximately 200,000 employees and an annual operating budget in excess of fifteen billion dollars.

redefine the objective so that nondelivery looks like a product or marshal together a persuasive set of arguments as to why a particular program could not be delivered in the first place.

A third common mistake of new chief executives is that they ignore or are unaware of commonsense administrative practice. This can manifest itself in one of two ways: too little administrative supervision (particularly of key agencies) or too much administrative interference.

Some agencies are simply more important than others by virtue of their size, the resources they command, or the scope of their authority. New chiefs—especially if they lack a personal interest in a particular program area—may leave major agencies too much to the discretion of the commissioner or manager. Failure to become involved with the agency, to get to know and work with the manager, may not mean that the agency suffers administratively but certainly means that that agency will have limited identification with the chief's goals and administration. If the agency does a terrific job, the chief will not get the proper credit; if the agency is scandalous, the chief will find out too late that all the blame rests at the chief's door, not the commissioner's. Finally, it is hard to retain good managers if the boss ignores them or appears to consider their operation unimportant. New chiefs often learn the hard way—by losing good people or by being blind-sided by a major scandal—that manager / chief relationships are a two-way, not one-way, street.

Too much administrative interference can be equally problematic. Chiefs who make a habit of diving directly into mid-management without the knowledge or cooperation of the agency head may seriously jeopardize relationships with their appointees. While at first it may appear that executive prerogatives allow the chief to order anyone at any level to do anything, a certain amount of administrative orderliness and protocol is necessary to manage an enterprise as complicated as government.

Sooner or later good chief executives realize that management is important and that implementation is hard and takes work and attention. Good chiefs learn to distinguish between managers who produce and managers who pretend. For the public manager, the time from election until this insight is gained may be trying. Maintaining a good relationship with the chief during this period is a real skill; managing well at the same time is a real challenge.

PUBLIC MANAGERS, CHIEFS, AND BOSSES: INTERACTION AND CONFLICTS

Public managers and their bosses deal with each other all of the time, on many issues and in many different situations. Sometimes these interactions lead to support for the manager's programs, sometimes to debate and conflict, and sometimes to a flat-out no.

Regardless of the character of the outcome, certain reasons for interacting are predictable. Policy setting, interagency disputes, legislative affairs, political relations, media relations, arguments between personal staff and agency staff, and problems with community or other interest groups all force chiefs and agency heads to deal directly with each other. Public managers learn quickly that their scorecard on these occasions—winning or losing the chief's respect and support—determines how much they can accomplish and how effectively they can manage. Anticipating the circumstances under which a manager is likely to conflict with the chief or the boss is half the battle.

Points of potential friction

POLICY   Public managers understandably want to have the main voice in developing policy that affects their own agency. In order to do so effectively the manager must have access to the chief, must be an accepted part of the administration's policy development process, and must be offensive as well as defensive in putting forth the agency's program.

For a variety of reasons, however, chief executives may want primary control of policy matters. They may wish to consult other officials, outside experts, and personal staff in addition to the public manager, or to make policy pronouncements without consulting the responsible agency heads. These situations typically annoy and confuse the manager and lead to predictable, if temporary, conflicts with the boss.

OVERHEAD AGENCIES   Any public manager who is responsible for a line agency knows well that disputes with overhead agencies—on budget, personnel, and procurement—consume enormous amounts of time and frequently end up in the chief's lap. These disputes are such an important part of the manager's environment that the next chapter is devoted entirely to them.

The reason for conflict with overhead agencies is simple: the objectives and priorities of an overhead agency—to hold the line, save money, and keep the payroll within reason—are in fundamental conflict with the needs and demands of agency managers. These disputes lead in part to efficiency and accountability in government, in part to a serious set of obstacles for the public manager.

For a variety of reasons explored in Chapter 3, overhead agencies may not uniformly honor the requests of line managers. Bureaucratic infighting is the order of the day, and to win in the trenches (at least a respectable amount of the time) the manager badly needs the support of the chief, or at least a reputation for being able to get that support. The appearance of support may be sufficient to settle disputes short of chief executive intervention, but once inside the chief's office that support had better be very real.

Chiefs frequently become arbiters (often to their displeasure) of manager / overhead agency disputes. Overhead agencies usually have the advantage when the argument gets this far. They have an aura of power; they approach problems from a less parochial perspective than the line manager (they have the "big picture"); and they have more regular contact with the chief than do their operating agency counterparts. Conflicts with overhead agencies that regularly require the intervention of the chief executive are bound to undermine the public manager. A good manager learns how to avoid them.

OTHER LINE AGENCIES   Just as it is predictable that managers will have disputes with overhead agencies so will they have conflicts with their line-agency colleagues. More often than not these skirmishes will involve conflicts over policy matters or disputes about jurisdiction.

Policy disputes among government agencies are as certain as the sun rising in the morning. Different agencies have different goals, legitimately conflicting missions, and overlapping spheres of influence. The police want Johnny locked up, the public defender wants him off, and the social service department wants him to themselves; the Defense Department wants intervention, the National Security Council wants harsh pronouncements, and the State Department wants to have tea with the same misbehaving ally. The opportunities for interagency disputes are endless; and, once again, the chief executive becomes the mediator, arbitrator, even dictator in such debates.

Jurisdictional disputes between line agencies also occur regularly. New York City decides to start a new health care program in the prisons. Who runs it—the Health Department or the Department of Correction? The governor wants to consolidate all environmental functions in a single agency by pulling bits and pieces from several existing operations. The new agency head tries to get as much as possible; the old agency heads try to hold onto their turf.

Whether it is a jurisdictional or a policy dispute, line managers find themselves in the position of competing for resources, power, influence, and, once again, the chief's support. Public managers should anticipate such conflict, especially when they introduce new programs which could be implemented in different ways. The ultimate disposition of any issue may depend as much on the manager's personal relationship with the chief as on the substance of the debate.

THE CHIEF'S STAFF The characteristics of the chief's personal staff may be an important factor in dealings with the chief. In some governments this is not much of an issue for the agency head because the personal staff is small and has clearly defined responsibilities. In others, however, the staff can be the bane of the manager's life.

Some chiefs build enormous personal staffs with extensive and varied authority: press aides, legal counsel, appointments personnel, as well as program specialists, staff with monitoring and evaluation responsibilities, and staff with supervisory authority over line agencies.

The size of the chief's personal staff is not the critical

factor in determining its quality or power. A small staff can wield enormous power while a big staff may be unimportant; the reverse may also be true. While there are many good reasons for chief executives to have them, strong staffs are far from a pure blessing for the public manager. Strong staffs mean predictable conflicts over access to the chief and over policy matters and internal agency management. Strong staffs can also mean extra resources, badly needed objectivity and perspective, and productive liaison for the agency head or other public manager.

Staff aides often limit the agency heads' access to the chief executive. Sometimes this is legitimate; the chief simply cannot see every government manager every time the manager believes it necessary. But as often as not this restricted access represents the desire on the part of staff members to enhance their personal power and keep every issue within their own bailiwick. Internal office politics—the one who spends the most time with the boss is perceived as the most powerful—contributes to this tendency. The same situation often occurs with respect to "policy." Staff aides may insist that policy initiatives or problems be cleared with them first before any presentation to the chief is allowed.

Particularly at the state and local level, bright, energetic, often inexperienced young staff aides may think they can run an agency from city hall or from the governor's mansion. They want to get heavily involved in internal administrative matters—personnel decisions, budget changes, program alterations. They like the power they have—often the first taste of it in their lives; it is heady stuff for a twenty-five-year-old to tell an experienced manager what to do. The best of them understand that you cannot operate a government for long this way and that it is in the chief's best interest to have a strong agency head exercising day-to-day control. But there are plenty of aides who never get this message.

Staff aides frequently have substantial power, and this may result—particularly with the young ones—in a touch of arrogance. Aides who are arrogant and self-righteous are not likely to be charming on any level. The fact that they often combine arrogance with inexperience can be not merely irritating but damaging to the public manager. Aides may unfairly evaluate the public manager's performance and report back to the boss. Without contrary evidence the chief is likely to accept these negative judgments at face value, assuming that the staff aide is trying to evaluate problems from the chief's perspective.

Another common problem of young staffers is that they are not nice to people. Several at City Hall who revered Lindsay were well known for their lack of tact and common courtesy. This is bad for several reasons. For one thing, it's bad on the merits. For another, such behavior flies in the face of what should be an aide's prime objective—namely, to put himself or herself in the boss's shoes and make the boss look good. When staff aides are nasty to people, the one who pays in the end is the boss, particularly if he is a politician and is, by definition, in the business of trying to make people like him.

Since that's the case, it is curious how frequently this sort of problem occurs. New York clearly did not invent it. I saw plenty of the same in the Kennedy White House, and Nixon's staff men reached a new low.

When President Kennedy was assassinated, the change of guard at the White House was very

*noticeable to me. As a young staff man myself, I
was struck by the difference between the two sets
of aides. Johnson's men—people like Jack Valenti
and Bill Moyers—were as bright as the Kennedy
people, but their style was different. They treated
people better. In Kennedy's days there was a sort
of myth about efficiency and toughness. There was
no idle chatter. It was a contest to see who could
say the most in the shortest time and in the fewest
words. Many of them simply weren't nice people.*

INTERNAL AGENCY MANAGEMENT   Staff aides are
not the only ones who cause problems in internal agency
management; chiefs often get a hand in it themselves.

The chief's attitude toward an agency head can affect the internal administration of the agency. If the
chief is not supportive, agency morale can decline, new
staff will be harder and harder to recruit, and the
critical battles with overhead agencies and legislatures
over money, jobs, and facilities will be lost more often
than won.

Chiefs are more likely to engage themselves (or their
staff) in day-to-day agency matters in a time of crisis.
Virtually all chiefs will take crisis management seriously and become deeply engrossed in agencies facing
major problems. The chief has a political incentive to
become involved as much for the symbolic as for the
substantive value.

The impact of crisis situations and a chief's involvement can be great, both on the manager and on the
agency. Often there is a role reversal in such circumstances, with the chief executive seeking assistance
from the manager in order to "fix" the problem. Very
often the chief needs symbolic actions to demonstrate
that something is being done, like the firing of certain
personnel or the issuance of an investigative report. If

not justified (and sometimes even when they are), such actions can drive a wedge between the manager and the manager's subordinates. Members of the bureaucracy will trust the manager less if they believe that decisions in a crisis situation are being made more for the chief's political expediency than for the good of the agency or its employees.

Conflicts between managers and chiefs can also occur if the chief tolerates or encourages end runs by the manager's staff. No agency head likes to have a subordinate say, "But we have to do it this way. I've already checked with the governor. . . ."

Just as managers and chiefs can clash over internal agency affairs, they can also work to each other's benefit. Chiefs can be extremely helpful in recruitment, in bolstering agency morale through public recognition from the chief's office, and in publicizing agency accomplishments (and not coincidentally the manager's successes).

JOBS AND PATRONAGE Public managers, their bosses, and chief executives interact and often collide over jobs and patronage. Managers want to staff their own agencies but chief executives often have different ideas. The issue can be joined over both high- and low-level appointments.

On high-level jobs the chief may have both political and personal reasons for wanting to retain control over appointments. The chief may need to use the personnel process to mollify certain constituencies and interest groups, or the chief may have administrative reasons for hiring a particular person—to shore up a weak agency head, or to provide a direct line of contact to agencies whose heads are considered controversial or potentially disloyal.

For the public manager such high-level intervention

can be particularly troubling. It is hard to run an agency effectively if your immediate deputies are not of your own choosing. Frequently such appointees will be less responsive to requests and orders from the manager than would otherwise be the case. While this problem is more common at the federal level where the president retains control over hundreds of appointments, it also happens in state and local government.

When agency heads—particularly at the state and local level—and chiefs argue about low-level positions, the issue is generally not one of controlling the agency but rather one of patronage and political rewards. Patronage is commonplace everywhere. In some places managers have little or no control over the hundreds of low-level jobs available—these are parceled out by the chief, or in some cases legislatures or party organizations. In other jurisdictions patronage is relatively rare, and the agency head may get no more than a few requests a year. In areas where the patronage system is strongly rooted in tradition—and that tradition is embraced by the elected chief—conflicts over these low-level jobs may become especially tiresome.

MEDIA   Concerning media the source of problems between manager and chief is simple: the chief wants the good press and wants the manager to take the bad.

Chiefs like good copy; they want it, they need it, and they appreciate it. Chiefs generally do not like agency heads who get good press on their own—without appropriate references to their boss and their boss's administration. Chiefs do not like surprises with their morning coffee—especially if the story involves a scandal, failure, or other controversy.

Agency heads have legitimate reasons for wanting good press. Unlike chief executives, public managers rarely seek good stories for electoral purposes, but the objective is political nonetheless. As is discussed in more detail in Chapter 6, public managers want a good public image for their programs and services. A reputation for effectiveness and competence comes with a good public relations effort, and this helps in all the manager's relationships, both inside and outside of government.

Public managers and chiefs handle this natural competition for media coverage in a variety of ways. Some managers simply accede to the chief's wishes and do not seek coverage for themselves. Others may feed enough stories to the chief's press office to keep them happy but still save one or two choice pieces for themselves. Others simply "do their own thing," trying to persuade their bosses that stories emanating from within the agency have more credibility than stories prepared outside. These arguments may have merit, but they are frequently not persuasive to chiefs who know the political significance of headlines and airtime; it is, after all, the chief who stands for election, not the manager.

Other manager / chief interactions on the media are less strained. At times agency heads look to their chief to get publicity for services or programs that might otherwise be overlooked. A governor publicizing a new campaign against child abuse will attract much more attention than an agency social worker doing the same thing. The chief's visibility and command of media attention can be a helpful instrument for many of the manager's program initiatives.

Chiefs may also use the media as a management tool—a way to talk directly to the bureaucracy or to certain constituent groups about policy or the administration's plans. Sometimes press conferences and other media instruments are used to expedite particular programs—to make clear the chief's commitment to action and desire to move sluggish agencies. If this is done with the manager's concurrence, it can aid internal agency management; if, on the other hand, the manager is the one being goaded, it may well lead to conflict.

One thing that struck me about the City Hall press was its difference from the White House press, in at least one respect. Anyone working for the federal government recognizes the frequency with which presidential public announcements are used to set policy and goals for the federal bureaucracy.

It was quite normal for the president to try to move a lumpen bureaucracy by announcing publicly that such and such department will complete such and such goal by a certain date. What the president is doing, in effect, is using the press as a management tool—that is, putting the department on the hook to deliver by making it likely that they will look bad if they don't. The publicity in a sense is an incentive.

It is very different in New York. While a mayor may try as hard as he can to dissociate himself from some event, New Yorkers simply won't let him do it, even though, on the merits, he may have had less control over a situation than Kennedy had at the Bay of Pigs. And I suspect that the experiences of state and local chief political executives, in this regard, are more like the New York City mayor's than the president's.

With the game played the New York way, the political executive is less likely to use the press as a management tool to goad his departments and more likely to make sure that a goal is really reachable before announcing it publicly. He knows that if he puts an agency chief's head on the hook, his own will be on it also, whether he likes it or not.

Another difference between the White House and City Hall was the press briefing for the principal before a press conference. When I was at the White House, a presidential press conference called for elaborate preparation. All agencies submitted in notebook form the questions that they thought likely to be asked, the background of the issue, and a suggested reply. While the purpose of this was in fact to prepare the president for the press conference, it had a spin-off which was useful to the president in management terms. In effect, it caused the agencies to reveal their problems. And it was usually successful, because there was nothing more embarrassing to an agency than to have some reporter nail the president on a subject that the agency had not prepared him for.

The mayor did not get this sort of preparation on the problems of city agencies. It would have been a full-time job for each agency to do this, since the mayor is accessible to the press formally and informally many times a week (for example, almost every time he walks out of his office, no hordes of security men surrounding him). He does not have the luxury of being able to call press conferences at his choosing once a month or so and remaining relatively isolated from the press in between these conferences. Thus, the mayor of New York—as well as governors and other mayors—has to learn to be fast on his feet, if he isn't already by the time he has the job.

LEGISLATIVE RELATIONS   One of the most sensitive areas in which managers and chiefs interact is legislative relations. Agency heads generally need action by the legislature to achieve (or establish) program objectives. Here the chief's support can be crucial.

The chief can assist by supporting and promoting the

manager's legislative recommendations. Agency heads compete to get their new programs and policies incorporated into the chief's annual legislative package. The agency head who consistently obtains the chief's support for these legislative initiatives has probably established a good relationship on all other scores as well; the public manager who is less successful had better think twice about how things are going with the front office. The problem does not end when the legislation is introduced. There is competition as well between agencies for the chief's lobbying efforts and attention. The chief's lobbying time is scarce—both because of time constraints and because the chief can only go to the well every so often. Everything cannot have priority, and a chief (or manager) who puts each desired piece of legislation on an urgent basis frequently gets nothing. But the chief's lobbying power is an extremely important resource for the manager, as the chief is likely to be far more effective with the legislature than is the agency head. Of course, bad relations between chief executives and legislative bodies are not rare, and such situations may provoke more than a little conflict between chiefs and managers about how legislative agendas are to be pursued.

POLITICAL RELATIONS   Public managers like to consider themselves professionals, not politicians. But being a good politician is part of the job; because this is true, political relations provide still another potential source of friction for chief executives and their managers. Managers play politics a lot—in fact, most of their dealings with the environment involve political strategy. But conflicts occur when the chief and the manager promote different ends, or when one agency outperforms another in harnessing the chief's political energy.

Chiefs may adopt certain policies or promote certain programs primarily for political reasons. When such initiatives are inconsistent with a manager's overall view of the best way to deliver services or manage programs, conflict may result.

Similarly, the chief (as well as the manager) frequently exercises discretion as to whether to provide or withhold certain programs, facilities, or services—for example, in situations where a number of communities are eligible for a given development but only one can be chosen. In these cases politics plays a key role, and a manager insensitive to political dynamics may end up on the short end of the stick, or in a public debate with the chief, or bypassed altogether in the line of final decision. Public managers would obviously prefer that such discretionary decisions come out their way, and here again they find themselves in competition with their colleagues. The agency head who has clout with the chief is much more likely to win on these issues than one who does not.

A public manager also needs the chief's support in other political matters; the manager may need protection from a political rival who is using the manager as a proxy for the chief. The manager may need the political support of a key legislator to get a controversial program opened in the legislator's district, or the manager may simply need some political muscle to fend off an aggressive interest group or community organization. In all of these cases the chief may be in a much better position to handle the problem than is the public manager. Being able to count on that support, without the fear of finding yourself standing alone, is crucial to your survival as a public manager.

OUTSIDE GROUPS   Finally, public managers and chief executives will interact and conflict on issues involving outside groups: unions, community organizations, special-interest groups, and similar organizations. The chief's support can make dealing with these outside forces considerably easier and less unpleasant for the public manager.

Public managers often require the cooperation of outside groups to implement programs. The public manager who is perceived to be a close colleague of the chief may gain this needed cooperation quickly; the manager who is weak and is considered out of favor with the chief executive normally will not. These external groups simply will not view the manager's agenda as important without the imprimatur of the elected chief, unless they are publicly at odds with the chief and out to promote conflict within the administration.

The chief also has an intense interest in managers' relationships with politically influential outside groups. For example, the interests clustered around highway construction—landowners, contractors, truckers, etc.— are so considerable that any chief (federal, state, or local) will watch carefully to see how the transportation director deals with those interests (and the chief's political future). No chief wants public managers who are considered "anti-community," and few chiefs will sit by quietly if managers are creating problems or acting capriciously with politically important outside interests. Conversely, managers who can deliver on these relationships will hold a particularly warm spot in a politically ambitious chief's heart.

All of these areas—staff, policy, press, community groups, overhead agencies, line agencies—make up the business of public manager / chief executive relationships. The interests of the manager and the chief or boss are inextricably linked in each case. The trick is to make sure that the interests of both the manager and the boss are one and the same more often than not.

THE CARE AND FEEDING OF
BOSSES AND CHIEF ELECTED OFFICIALS

To be effective the public manager must know how to gain the chief's support and maintain the chief as an ally. The personalities, powers, and problems outlined above suggest some ground rules for establishing the all-important relationship between the chief or boss and the manager.

Establish good personal relations.

It almost goes without saying that a prudent agency head will want to be on good personal terms with the chief elected official. Best of all, of course, is a warm, longstanding, mutually respectful friendship which assures easy access and open communication. This does not mean cronyism but instead the kind of mutual respect that develops between competent professionals of long association. But this is an unusual situation for most public managers, and normally agency heads will have to settle for building a personal relationship with the chief from the ground up.

Being responsive and quick in replying to the chief's large or small requests, being courteous and coopera-tive with the chief's political allies and personal friends (many of whom involve themselves during transition periods), and being civil and cooperative with the chief's new staff aides will help to establish the public manager as an eager team player and reliable col-league. Obviously, these efforts must be coupled with good judgment and substance. Not team play for its own sake, but team play to help meet a common objective.

Some public managers go even further, hanging around city hall or the statehouse, "leaning on fenders," chatting with staff aides, and otherwise ingratiating themselves to the new order. This strategy is not recommended. It is a time waster, and sooner or later the people in power are going to begin wondering who is back home minding the manager's agency. When good personal friendships do not already exist between a manager and a chief when the chief takes office, they are more likely to be formed as a result of demonstrated ability rather than "good time Charlie" and "hail fellow well met" routines.

Perform, deliver, produce.

In the end the only basis for a solid professional relationship between a public manager and a chief executive is performance. The single most important thing that an agency head can do to gain the chief's support is to demonstrate—as soon after the chief takes office as possible—that the manager can deliver; that when a policy or program is to be implemented, it can be done quickly and professionally at reasonable cost and with high quality.

Agency heads who meet these criteria are few and far between, but those who do will be cherished by their chiefs. They will be the ones the chief turns to in a crisis or to solve a problem, or the ones the chief helps when money is up for grabs. The chief's future depends in part on these managers' performance. Congressional representatives may be able to run on what they say, but incumbent chief executives have to run on what they do or have done, and for that they are dependent on (or at the mercy of) their cadre of appointees.

While little impresses chiefs as much as an agency head who can actually get something implemented in the public sector, a public manager can demonstrate competence in other ways as well.

The public manager should be an initiator of policy,

not just a reactor to other people's ideas and initiatives. Because the manager is the "expert" and has the time and staff available to research, plan, and create new programs, the manager should be way ahead of the chief in his or her own area. Managers who know less about their programs than the chief executive does either have very, very smart bosses or aren't very good themselves.

Managers should never present a problem to the chief without at least some proposed solution. There is little more infuriating to superiors than subordinates who elegantly outline the obstacles being faced without suggesting some means of getting around, over, or through them.

And then of course there is money. A sure-fire way to get your chief to stand up and take notice, to endear yourself to your boss, is to find sources of revenue outside of the chief's own treasury. Skilled grant writers and creative fiscal managers can be the apple of the governor's eye, assuming, of course, that the creativity and the revenue raising are legal, carefully handled, and scandal-proof.

At least appear competent, even if all is not perfection.

If clothes make the man, then the appearance of competence and the ability to communicate performance are almost as good as the real thing. It is incredible how many otherwise talented public managers (to say nothing of clearly untalented public managers) communicate the opposite of competence and ability by their demeanor, speech, and written work. The way a meeting with the chief is handled, the way a report or proposal is presented, the way a TV interview appears—all reflect on the agency as well as the manager and consciously and unconsciously create a lasting image in the chief's mind.

It is important, for example, to handle meetings with the chief carefully; to be fully prepared, to limit the retinue of staff, and to be briefed well enough to present your own defense. As a general rule it is good for the manager to make his or her own case, deferring to "expert" staff for amplifications, specific details, and technical points. There are undoubtedly exceptions to this rule, but beware of getting into the habit of letting your staff control your interchanges with the chief; if you do, you will pretty quickly appear superfluous. It is also important, however, to be sure that substantive differences, alternative scenarios, and all potential consequences are clearly laid before the chief. To the extent that professional subordinates hold dissenting views and can present such alternatives succinctly, they can be used to the manager's advantage.

The real essence of appearing competent is for managers to demonstrate that their agency is special—that they do good things that other agencies do not do and that they set standards that other agencies would do well to follow.

In New York, for example, I used to prepare and circulate two types of administrative reports, one a biweekly progress report of each major agency in the department and the other a six-month update on the department as a whole and overall progress toward our goals and objectives. There was no requirement to furnish these reports, but they were extremely useful and well received; they provided facts and figures but didn't dwell exclusively on how many meetings we'd had, or how many community groups we'd delivered—instead they focused on how many people we'd helped to make healthy that two-week or four-week or six-month period. It distinguished the agency and set it apart, both in tone and in performance, from other city offices. No one knew how closely they were read in City Hall, but everyone seemed to like the fact that they existed. Needless to say, fellow administrators may not like such attention-grabbing tactics, particularly if they are things which good management dictates should be done anyway; but vying for the chief's support in order to maintain agency resources and enhance program effectiveness is a competitive business, and no one is stopping fellow managers from being high achievers themselves.

In addition to formal reports and transmissions, there are other, less structured ways to spread the news about your agency and its achievements. If you are attracting particularly high-quality talent, let the chief know, get the people introduced, let them "strut their stuff" a bit. If you have a spectacular program going and clients are enthusiastic, encourage them to get the word to city hall. Mayors', governors' and presidents' mail baskets are rarely filled with kudos for government performance. If a client, colleague, or associate is inclined to pat you on the back, get those congratulations routed to the boss's desk. They will do a lot more good there than in your in-box.

Educate the chief about management; feed information in the way the chief prefers, not just a way you find convenient.

Any agency manager spends a good deal of time educating bosses and chief executives and their staffs. Managers must communicate the problems of administration, the often complex substance of programs and policies, and the way agency operations relate to other government priorities and actions.

Unfortunately, educating bosses is not easy, and it is a common source of mistakes by public managers. You simply must find out, early on, how your boss likes to receive information and how he or she best absorbs it: written memos? briefings? short summaries? long research reports? in sections? all at once? at regular meetings? or in informal communication?

Unless you are providing information to the boss in such a way that he or she will use it, your time and effort will be wasted. Elected chiefs, especially new ones, may not know how to assimilate the vast amount of information that travels through any executive's office. You may have to experiment, with both of you learning together how best to communicate.

The chief's or boss's staff may help with this. More than the chief they will be available for early consultation, will be familiar with their own trial and error in getting through to the boss, and will be sensitive to the best timing for introducing various issues. Involvement of key staff in initial policy making can lead to their increased interest and support. This allows easier access to the chief and guarantees a friendly voice in close proximity to the chief's ear. Moreover, this can help to preclude some of the arguments that will develop inevitably with the chief's staff.

Good communication is a highly personal art. No one can say with certainty what is the best way to prepare an administrative memorandum, design a briefing book, conduct a conference, or prepare correspondence. You must determine with your own chief and the chief's staff the preferred methods in your own situation. But remember to be flexible; what worked with your last boss may not work with the new one, and what works for your boss may not be your favorite way of presenting things. Above all, make sure that you know what you are talking about regardless of how it is presented. If you have little to say or do not know what it is you are proposing, it will make no difference how capably it is packaged.

Involve the chief in programs and projects.

Chief executives deal with literally thousands of programs and projects every year. Without prodding it is difficult to get them to exhibit proprietary interest in your agency and its programs—unless of course you manage an area that has been of longstanding interest to them.

Agency heads can sometimes encourage a chief's support by asking the chief to provide public or private assistance to get a project going, or by arranging for him or her to meet and talk with clients benefiting directly from a service. More than anything else, keeping the chief informed regularly about the progress of activities that have caught the chief's eye is important. Eliciting a proprietary interest on the part of the chief carries with it an obligation to keep updates flowing and to manage the program successfully.

Establish credibility with your peers.

Where conflict is predictable—on budget, policy, turf, personnel, and other resources—the perceived standing of an agency head with the chief may be as important with colleagues as the actual standing.

A reputation among executive branch peers that you win more than you lose when it comes down to a chief executive decision means that they will be reluctant to let any dispute get that far. A perceptive agency head will always weigh the probability of winning or losing before escalating a dispute to higher levels. Your credibility with your colleagues and your reputation for winning with the boss may tip the scales in your favor more often than not.

Agency heads are strongly inclined to settle disputes among themselves. Nobody likes to go running to the boss with a problem—especially on jurisdictional issues that are likely to annoy the chief because they are usually more form than substance. Your colleagues will be willing to compromise and look more favorably on your position if you refrain from heading toward the chief's office every time things get sticky and if you carefully cultivate your image as a professional as well as an intimate of the chief.

Early on in an administration, you should take a few issues to the chief on which you are absolutely certain you are right. Then continue—through anticipation, initiative, and competence— to solidify your reputation with your peers and retain control over decisions important to your agency.

Use your head with high-level vacancies; anticipate the chief's interests.

As much as possible it is important for managers to be able to choose (and fire) their immediate subordinates. While the temptation for the chief and the chief's staff to get involved in these decisions is great, it can be minimized with a little common sense.

First, do not keep high-level jobs open too long. It will encourage the chief's intervention and give interest groups, special constituencies, and other external players time to find and promote their own candidates. Furthermore, a longtime vacancy can give the impression that the job is either not important or not necessary and leave you vulnerable to attack by the overhead agencies, who will look for any opportunity to save money by eliminating superfluous high-level jobs.

Second, anticipate the political and constituent pressure on the chief in your own recruiting practices. Whenever possible, satisfy these concerns, but with your own candidate—not the chief's. If you consistently ignore the chief's interests with respect to geographic, ethnic, and political distribution of key employees, you deserve to have strangers rammed down your throat.

Third, when necessary, fight back. There is no reason why you have to lose every debate about hiring if you have an otherwise good working relationship with the chief. Be sparing, and stick to your guns only when you really believe that the job or candidate is worth your taking a stand. A reputation for uncooperativeness is easy to come by in manager / chief relationships and is a reputation the manager simply cannot survive. Going to the well once too often may make you look disloyal, not just persistent.

Of course the chief can also help to recruit good people for important positions. People who are looking for jobs in the public sector will frequently make it a point to find out which agency heads are in the chief's favor and which are not. The best people—the ones with many options—will stay away from agency heads who appear to be out of favor because that normally means fewer resources and a lower priority for the manager's programs (unless, of course, it looks like a good opportunity to move in and take over). The chief can also help attract people in a more active way, by being available if an agency head feels that a little personal attention from the chief is just the thing needed to attract a given candidate. Support from the chief in hiring and recruiting will also minimize end runs which can dilute a manager's authority and cut him or her out of the information flow. When the mayor or governor has made clear a commitment to the agency head, both new and old staff know better than to try to buck that relationship for their own ends.

Cooperate on low-level jobs, but set a few rules.

There is no point in losing sleep, or jeopardizing your relationship with the chief, over low-level positions. But a carte blanche for political patronage is untenable. Most agency heads learn to live with whatever patronage system seems to be in place in their government. But this does not mean that the manager needs to be a pushover when the chief's patronage dealer calls.

Agency heads may find that they can (at least they should try to) insist on certain rules: that the agency head picks the job (a person may be entitled to a job but not a specific job); that the employee must be minimally qualified and must work (that is, cannot be a no-show); and that patronage employees can be fired if they do not make the grade.

Above all, the agency head should keep score. An almost foolproof way of fending off the patronage dealer is by providing evidence that your agency is getting more than its share of patronage appointees or that the ones accepted so far have been unmitigated disasters. After all, fair is fair.

Draw limits on the chief's staff aides, but be cooperative.

Difficult, arrogant, and inexperienced staff can be kept under control with a little care. While the task is probably aggravating, the time it takes to draw limits and establish procedures for agency / staff interactions will pay off in the long run. Do not shut out staff aides just because they are irritating. Make sure they are included often enough to feel involved but not deeply enough to cause problems. Do not keep from them information that is going to get out anyway just to prove you are in charge.

Establish standard operating procedures with your subordinates and agency personnel on dealings with the chief's staff. Do not refuse to allow contacts, but make sure that they are reported to you and that your staff understands that no commitments can be made without your approval. Do not put your SOPs in writing—that will only give the appearance that you are trying to isolate your people from the aides.

Above all, keep an open mind. Your best defense in controlling ambitious but inexperienced staffers is to be professional and to know more than they do about your programs and services.

> *The ideal situation is to have your own staff aide "promoted" to be the boss's aide. I experienced this with Nat Leventhal, who moved from the Health Services Administration to be health assistant to Mayor Lindsay. I can't say I had him wrapped around my little finger, but we certainly had a better time of it than I was used to with other chief executives' aides.*

And be flexible; many of these staffers are capable and intelligent. If they are, use them; they can turn into real assets and can extend your own resources. Besides, it is better to have them on your side than against you.

Keep the boss informed.

Nothing is more likely to trigger an all-out assault on the manager's day-to-day administrative authority than letting the boss be taken by surprise.

While it would be nice for chief executives to spend all their time and effort on relationships with their managers, it simply is not possible. As a manager you will have to take the initiative to keep the chief informed on you and your agency's activities. Do not let the chief be the last to know when you are up against a problem or a potential crisis, or when you are about to initiate a major new program. When a crisis does occur, propose ways to keep the chief involved and find ways to make sure the chief gets the credit when the problem is resolved. Do not put the chief out front if you know there is going to be a disaster.

Give the good press to the chief and accept the fact that there will be precious little left over for you.

The rules on the media, you, and the chief are simple: give the good press to the boss; use the chief to publicize the stories that would not be covered unless the chief were involved; and never, never criticize the chief in public (or for that matter, in private—it is bound to get back).

Keep the chief well briefed on agency programs, and provide ample warning when you know a bombshell is about to drop. Better yet, make sure you get up earlier every morning than the chief does. If the headline is bad, it had better be you who breaks the news and not the chief of staff or an incensed political colleague of the boss.

The corollary: take the heat.

Public managers should be careful not to foist problems off on their bosses solely to avoid taking public blame. A chief does not have to be very smart to know when an agency head is ducking an issue in order to be able to tell an angry community group or constituent that the adverse decision was the chief's, not the manager's. Of course on some issues buck-passing is necessary, but at least it should be discussed with the chief beforehand and a plan of action mutually agreed upon.

By and large, public managers need to acquire thick skins and broad shoulders to absorb as much of the responsibility as possible for the less popular but necessary decisions that make government work. It is a lot better for the manager to bite the bullet and the chief to say "Of course I stand by my manager" than it is for the manager to toss the bullet over for the chief to both bite and swallow.

Maintain your integrity; it is a necessary complement to loyalty.

Sooner or later every public manager faces a situation, in a conflict with a chief executive, where the matter is so serious that it is worth jeopardizing the manager's job, where the issue is one of personal or professional principle. In any working relationship it is important for both you and the boss to know, at least implicitly, what the limits are. Loyalty is not a great deal of help to a chief executive if it is not coupled with integrity. In fact, blindly loyal aides have pulled down a great many more chief executives than have managers who found it necessary to resign on principle. You have to make your own judgments about where and when to draw the line between your obligation to your chief and your professional judgments about policy.

The worst mistake you can make as a manager is to take issue with an order and, staying in the job, go out and publicize your disagreement without warning the chief of your action. If it comes to that point, you should either implement the chief's decision or find a more compatible boss. There is little room for "in between."

In summary, if you cannot (or do not want to) get the chief on your side, be prepared to dramatically lower your expectations about what can be accomplished. Constantly assess and reassess your chief's political and management power and style, and be sensitive to political as well as substantive issues. If your chief executive does not yet understand the importance of management and implementation, then you will have to find ways to break bureaucratic bottlenecks on your own.

With a rookie chief elected official, be helpful, constructive, and responsive. With a seasoned one, be (in addition) astute, politically sensitive, and above all competent. If you produce, you will be ninety percent of the way toward a good relationship with your boss and a solid foundation for all the other working relationships in the public manager's environment.

3 / Managers and Managers: Coping with Overhead Problems

Every government has its overhead agencies: agencies that deliver their services not to the public but to the government itself. Collectively these agencies form a necessary part of government, an overhead system that provides the infrastructure for government operations. Budget and fiscal agencies prepare the budget and oversee its administration. Personnel and civil service departments attempt to standardize pay levels and employee practices throughout the jurisdictions they serve. Other agencies exist to purchase equipment, acquire facilities, and obtain supplies and services for the government. When they work well—when line managers and overhead managers cooperate and collaborate—much can be accomplished.

But the gap between theory and practice, observed in many government activities, is never more obvious than in the case of the overhead system. In theory these agencies are designed to serve the executive branch; to aid the chief in allocating resources efficiently, consistent with the chief's policies; to ensure a competent, professional, and productive public work force; and to realize economies while maintaining quality in the construction of facilities, procurement of goods, and purchase of services. In practice the overhead agencies are often obstacles to efficient management in government. For the line manager they are important but sometimes troublesome facts of life. Much of what a manager can or cannot do is controlled by one or more of these agencies. In particular, the manager's ability to respond to changing public needs and circumstances can be severely constrained by the overhead system. The overheads are often the enemy within, which the manager must live with, combat, and conquer. Next to the chief executive they are the second most important determinant of success or failure in the manager's world.

THE NATURE OF OVERHEAD AGENCIES

One of the most important characteristics of the overhead system is that it is generally beyond public notice and scrutiny. Because of the complexity of the budget process, civil service regulations, and contracting procedures, the overhead agencies often seem mysterious and formidable. Because there is rarely direct contact between the public and these agencies—when was the last time John Doe requisitioned weekly groceries through the budget bureau?—there is little public interest and even less public accountability. Because the subject matter of overhead functions is often tedious—hardly sexy and rarely provocative—there is little about their activities to capture the public fancy. Except for an occasional scandal over kickbacks (and they tend to be whoppers because of the sums involved), the overhead system is rarely prime-time news.

The combination of complexity, obscurity, and tedium

means that overhead agencies can maintain an enviable isolation from accountability. When programs fail because they are underfunded, poorly staffed, or inadequately housed, it is the line manager who takes the fall, sometimes taking the chief executive down as well.

Battles between line agencies and the overhead system are inevitable; by nature they play conflicting roles. This conflict is over the lifeblood of government: money and personnel. The overhead system wants to give less and maintain control over what is given. The public manager wants to get more and increase his or her discretion. Only if one or both are asleep can conflict be avoided. When conflict happens, it can be bitter and defeat the intent and ability of even the best manager, especially if personalities also clash.

Defining the characteristics of overhead agencies, pointing out the major problems with them, and arming the manager for battle are the subject of this chapter.

BUDGET BUREAUS: POWERFUL PENNYPINCHERS OR CONSTRUCTIVE CONFEDERATES?

Budget bureaus perform two separate types of activities: budget preparation and budget administration (or oversight). While the process and procedures for each function vary from jurisdiction to jurisdiction, virtually all such agencies engage to some degree in both tasks.

Variations in the character and power of budget bureaus depend on a number of factors. The extent of the chief executive's explicit budget authority is one. The frequency and nature of the legislature's review is another. The frequency and complexity of the budget process itself—the number of transactions and people involved in any decision—is one of the most significant factors, and often determines whether the line manager views the budget as a cross to bear or a tolerable irritant—as rigorous or flexible.

The most clearcut differences between rigorous and flexible budget bureaus are found in their budget administration methods. Governments with overhead agencies retaining line-by-line budget controls are rigid, affording the public manager little or no discretion to modify, adjust, or alter resource allocation as circumstances require. Line-by-line methods specify each agency's budget by hundreds of individual items (in contrast to program budgets which specify larger sums by program area). Once an agency head gets that itemized budget, there can be no deviation without the budget agency's approval. If an administrator with a line item for a $15,000-per-year professional decides in the course of the year that two $7500 administrative assistants would be more productive, the budget agency must approve the switch. To exchange $2000 of budgeted typewriters that cannot be used for $2000 of adding machines that are desperately needed, the manager needs permission. It is a little like raising your hand to go to the bathroom: the consequences of being told no are understood by all parties, and nine times out of ten just getting up to go would be less disruptive. But the teacher insists on the rule to demonstrate authority and retain control. Public management is not a profession for persons with weak kidneys.

Less rigid but still cumbersome budget methods impose categorical controls. These systems allow the line manager discretion to modify the budget within categories—to turn typewriters into adding machines or program analysts into secretaries. Nevertheless, these systems continue to limit the manager's ability to amend or modify between categories. While somewhat more palatable to the public manager, even categorical budget administration retains in the overhead system the major decisions essential to effective management: How much will I spend? How many people will I use? When will I do it?

The most flexible and (from the manager's view) desirable budget systems differentiate the overhead agency's responsibility to "hold the line" from the public manager's responsibility to provide a service. The federal system is typical of these more flexible methods.

> *If you run an agency in Washington you have two basic constraints—a personnel ceiling and an appropriation level. Within these constraints you can administer your budget pretty much as you see fit. The Office of Management and Budget keeps track of your expenditures throughout the year, and if you start to overspend you're in trouble. But if you feel that you have to beef up one part of your operation at the expense of another—and if you're not getting paid to make that kind of a decision, what are you being paid for?—you can do it without a million pieces of paper and endless wrangles with the budget bureau.*

Also important, particularly in terms of constraints the budget imposes on a manager's discretion, is the proportion of the agency's revenue which is included in the formal development and review process. Often federal grants or other revenue sources external to the jurisdiction are less carefully scrutinized or even excluded from the allocation and distribution of locally generated monies. When this is the case, the manager can increase his or her discretion and control by increasing the proportion of outside resources in the budget.

The problems with budget bureaus begin with a conceptual dilemma. These agencies can operate from one of two perspectives: as keeper of the purse (doing everything possible to limit expenditure, program merit notwithstanding) or as promoter of the chief's policies (holding the line but ensuring that adequate resources are available for priority policies, programs, and services).

Typically, budget agencies think in the short term with dollars and positions unrelated or only marginally related to program services, quality, and objectives. Public managers generally prefer the other view. Budget bureaus that see themselves as policy staff to the chief can help to make decisions reflecting all concerns, not just the fiscal. Unfortunately this enlightened approach to the budget is rare, and political chiefs are forced to build up personal staffs to do the policy job for them. The more governments face retrenchment, however, the more the policy onus gets placed on the budget makers!

Because budget agencies are not accountable directly for the success or failure of any program, or for the implementation of new policies and services, they can easily survive with a "purse string" mentality. Chief political executives expect the budget agency to hold the line; and, especially if they are new and lack management experience, chiefs often do not equate the budget bureau's short-term decisions with the public manager's long-term performance and responsibility.

Some public managers are in more enviable positions than others relative to the budget process. Those whose agencies generate revenue are likely to warm the cockles of Scrooge's heart and enjoy an easier path with the budget bureau. Those whose functions involve more spending than earning—typically the case with human services—are likely to have the more difficult time.

PERSONNEL: NEITHER CIVIL NOR SERVICE

Personnel agencies handle issues fundamental to management control: who can be hired, who can be fired, who is promoted, and how much each is paid. Normally managers will want as much control over these decisions as possible, so that they can have the people they want and wield the carrot and stick to control them and ensure performance. Typically, however, the public manager will find few of these decisions within his or her authority. In some jurisdictions these decisions rest with or are heavily influenced by the legislature. In most, however, some or all of the agency's employees will fall under civil service regulations or collective bargaining agreements that define how recruiting occurs, who is qualified, what the job is, and how it is compensated. The manager's flexibility is a function of the complexity of the personnel rules and the percentage of employees they cover. The more complex the rules and the greater the percentage of employees covered, the more rigid the system.

Even for those jobs technically under the manager's control, there is usually a required civil service approval over the candidate and the candidate's salary. Much of the manager's time, therefore, will be spent trying to change, bend, or modify the personnel restrictions imposed by overhead agencies.

Personnel systems characteristically have several weaknesses. More often than not the hiring process involves an interminable number of steps and a great amount of time. Paperwork and delay have an inevitable consequence across jurisdictions: good people seek nongovernment opportunities rather than contend with the frustration of the hiring process. You may be able to snow bright young recruits with the majesty of your title and the awesome burden of your office, but the veneer of invincibility quickly wears thin if it takes six months to get them on board and their first paycheck is twenty-five percent less than they expected! These are the problems that tend to equalize managers: if you are a genius and cannot get a staff position filled, you are no better than the buffoon who cannot do it either. The ability to design a good program is considerably different from the ability to implement it; and the ability to implement depends more than anything else on the right staff.

Irrelevant standards

Other common weaknesses of personnel systems include their reliance on qualifying examinations (rarely validated to job performance) and on exaggerated, misleading, or irrelevant standard job descriptions. "Objectivity," in the form of standardization, is the backbone of the civil service philosophy. While such an approach may work well with routinized and technically specialized jobs, it often fails miserably with the more ambiguous, policy-oriented positions. Defining the job of a sanitation engineer and predicting the skills required to do it adequately are far different exercises from developing a job description and evaluating qualifications for a regional human services administrator. Similarly, testing for those skills necessary to be a competent lab technician is a more comprehensible task than testing for management or supervisory ability. Unfortunately, personnel systems, in the interests of equity, tend to apply the methods successful with simpler, less complex jobs across the board. It is a process notoriously short on introspection.

Personnel and civil service systems frequently have internal inequities required by law or enforced by tradition. Veterans' preference, emphasis on tenure within the civil service as opposed to education and experience outside of it, a common preference for hiring within rather than encouraging lateral transfer from agency to agency or jurisdiction to jurisdiction—all have the effect of discouraging competition and limiting the manager's ability to hire the best person for each specific job. Affirmative action and equal employment opportunity have reduced the exclusivity of civil service somewhat, but even so these personnel systems are still based on rigid regulations which make it tough to get in, keep you well protected once in, and make it damned difficult to be fired.

Reward and punishment

The most serious weakness of personnel systems is that they constrain the manager's ability to reward good work on one hand (employee incentives) and discipline poor performance on the other. Either the major incentive—money—is not available due to budget constraints, or its award is a presumed right basically unrelated to job performance. Annual merit increases, longevity pay, cost of living raises are usually structured in such a way that the burden of proof is on the manager to show why an employee is *not* entitled, rather than why an employee's performance merits reward. Too often the norm for government performance—"it's good enough for government work"—is at a minimum level rather than a good or superior one. If you come to work every day, do not abuse leave policy, do the minimum required, and do not rock the boat, you have performed satisfactorily and your annual merit increase is deserved.

The lack of viable incentives, the perversion over time of the civil service philosophy from one designed to ensure competence to one that protects mediocrity, and the problems of differential compensation (both higher and lower) offered to public sector employees in comparison with their private sector counterparts combine to make the task of recruiting the best and most talented people, and then retaining and promoting them, one of the manager's most challenging tasks. Refusing to be done in by these constraints is one of the surest signs of public management talent.

GOODS AND SERVICES: THE GOVERNMENT'S GENERAL STORE

The last major segment of the overhead system involves those agencies responsible for purchasing, procurement, maintenance, and construction and acquisition of facilities. These agencies are intended to serve government by providing the nonpersonnel resources necessary to conduct the government's business: the space, the equipment, the supplies, and the contracts.

While many public managers do not have to spend much time on problems with the general service agency, when such problems do crop up they can determine program success or failure. After all the other overhead hurdles, when a program is ready to go, there is nothing more frustrating than to find out that the facility you wanted cannot be rented for six months or that you will be ten weeks without phones, desks, or notepads when you are supposed to be running a hotline.

Because these agencies handle enormous sums of money, they can be targets for graft and corruption. While on the surface performing rather dull functions, general services agencies can be enormous sources of power; the place where the pols, the dollars, and the outstretched hands come together.

Even though these agencies may not have the day-to-day impact on the public manager that their overhead colleagues do, the potential for corruption and ability to gum up the works at the last minute make delicate and skillful handling by the public manager a must.

OVERHEAD TACTICS: OR WHEN DID YES BECOME A FOUR-LETTER WORD?

Overhead agencies use a variety of tactics to frustrate the public manager and maintain control over money and people. The attitude of the people who run overhead agencies was made chillingly clear in a *New York Times* article on New York City's personnel system: "[The Personnel Department's Director of Classification] has a philosophy that is credo in the world of civil service middle management—'you start by saying no to the request'."

In fact it is worse than that. A simple and direct no to a request would be too civilized and rational for the typical overhead agency. A prompt no at the start, allowing the line manager to begin negotiating with the overhead agency at once, would be an improvement over what actually happens—no response at all or endless requests for more information. These roadblocks are always supported by coconspirators in the overhead system, because delay in hiring, postponement of expenditures, or one more round of bids to find a lower contractor is presumed to save money, which is the *raison d'être* of the overhead system.

By far the favorite overhead tactic is simply not to respond to an agency's request. The same *New York Times* article notes that requests considered unreasonable "invariably expire in her [Director of Classification] office's open air filing system." Apparently this is much easier than giving the kind of no that will stick.

And since it is the way almost all requests are handled, it drives most managers crazy.

> *Even if the public manager survives the no and no response routine, a last, almost unbeatable tactic awaits—the great deception. A simple game: the overhead agency tells the line agency staff they can have what they want and then intentionally does not give it to them. This can be done in several ways; after all, sabotaging policy decisions has almost reached the level of Olympic sport in government bureaucracy. The budget director meets with the agency head and, after uncountable explanations and pleas by the manager, finally agrees to the lead poisoning control program. Naturally, because time is precious, the director will leave it up to subordinates to "iron out the details." The odds are high that the staffers will interpret their boss's decision in a way unfavorable to the line agency; and, lo and behold, the control program of fifty health sanitarians and half a million dollars suddenly is transformed into one with a staff of three persons transferred from other positions in the agency, with one quarter of the necessary funding.*

Of course irresponsible game playing by the overhead agencies encourages irresponsible behavior on the part of the public manager. It is easy to ignore the manager's supervisory responsibility and "pass the buck" when you know the predictable overhead system response. If an employee who you do not believe deserves a raise comes to you for one, you as a good manager should have the guts to say no. In many governments you do not have to do that. You can say "sure" and pass the papers on over to the overhead system—confident that without pressure from you they will be lost forever and no raise will be provided.

In the short view overhead conservatism "saves money." The more rigid the overhead system (the more transactions required and the more people involved), the more hurdles there are. Some administrators guide their requests over the hurdles; others do not. The stamina and resourcefulness of the administrator are what count. In such systems the merits all too often become irrelevant as the process becomes an end in itself. For the uninitiated the experience is more than perplexing; it is confounding. For the seasoned public manager it is the part of the job that either finally wears you down to acquiescence or constantly recharges your batteries through sheer provocation.

PREDICTABLE CONFLICTS: ANTICIPATING THE BATTLEGROUND

All overhead systems present problems for the public manager. No matter how progressive, no matter how benign, these agencies always have some power which sensible managers would prefer to have themselves. The severity of the problems presented depends on the nature of the overhead system. Rigid systems require review and approval of nearly every manager's decision at nearly every stage; they control the process through line-item budgeting, highly centralized personnel systems, and extremely circumscribed contracting authority. Flexible systems leave much discretion to the manager in day-to-day agency administration and are controlled broadly by appropriation levels and personnel ceilings. They are also characterized by flexible hiring procedures, decentralized hiring authority, and relatively decentralized contracting authority.

Assessing the restrictiveness of your own system is the first step toward coping with the hurdles. Anticipating which issues will generate conflict, and why, is the second.

On the budget

The public manager and the overhead system are certain to meet during budget development. The primary function of the budget agency is to allocate scarce resources among competing interests. In this respect the agency acts as an arm of the chief executive. Obviously the line manager wants to increase the resources available: more money and more staff mean a greater ability to do what the agency is supposed to do, more new programs, greater satisfaction for the agency's constituency, and a more impressive record for the manager. But all other line managers will feel the same way, and all of their budget demands taken together will add up to more than the chief executive (with one eye on the next election) will want to impose in the form of new taxes. Few if any managers will get all they want, but some will lose less than others. How the manager handles the budget agency is an important part of that process, though it is far from the whole story; the making of the budget also involves the political chief, the legislature, and—often—powerful interest groups outside of the government.

Conflicts over budget administration are inevitable. Once a budget is approved, the overhead system stays in business by monitoring and oversight. In times of budget retrenchment and cutbacks the red tape gets even worse, and budget shops deserve the title of "the abominable 'no'-man of government."

Conflict over the administration of an already approved budget is routine. Now let's suppose an agency head is crazy enough, in the middle of a fiscal year, to start a new program. For that the overhead system brings out the big guns, and the fireworks really get started.

Regardless of whether the administrator tries to start the new program with the agency's own funds (reallocating existing resources) or, God forbid, seeks additional funds (an almost treasonous act), the overhead system will say no or at the very least reduce the scope, number of people, and level of people requested for the program. The whole burden of proof is on the public manager to show why a given program should be started. It is never on the overhead system to prove why not. In my four years as administrator of the New York Health Services Administration, there was not one instance when a new program idea was presented to the budget bureau and they responded with "Great. How can we help you?" Instead they set their nit-pickers to work figuring out every possible objection.

On staff and services

Conflicts over personnel are obvious and have been described previously. A simple rule is to anticipate conflict over every decision: selection, promotion, discipline, and assignment. With personnel it is not an occasional skirmish—it is constant, unending water torture.

Like personnel conflicts, public manager / general services conflicts will occur most often over selection: Who will the consultant be? What kind of facility is best? What kind of typewriter can I have? Which provider should be assigned which services? Normally the substance of the disputes will involve:

- the complexity of the process—are eleven reviews of a bid really necessary?
- the equity of the process—why was a certain firm selected, and is it just coincidence that the firm's president is the procurement director's cousin?
- the quality of services rendered—did we really just renew a contract with a group home that has a track record of beating kids?
- and, of course, cost.

Whether on budget, personnel, goods, or services, all of these disputes are predictable and require careful preparation and creative strategies.

COPING WITH THE OVERHEADS: BASIC RULES

The public manager's objectives, in dealing with the overhead system, are to extract the maximum amount of resources possible to facilitate management and program implementation. The manager wants the most money, the most people, the best facilities, and the least disruption because of overhead requirements. With flexible overhead systems the capable manager can usually accomplish these objectives through good sense, good humor, professionalism, and a respect for the rules—playing fair when fair play is returned.

In routinized systems the manager can usually get along by going along. Taking the time to justify requests in writing (providing a clear trail if disputes occur), staying within the generally accepted mission of the agency, and offering to find additional resources for the public coffers (grant funds, fees, volunteer services) will often keep the public manager in good stead with the overhead system. Coupled with a good relationship to the chief executive, in the right circumstances this approach will almost certainly pay off.

In rigid systems, however, where transactions are more numerous and the process less predictable (for example, when other executive branch politicians or the legislature has a major role in the process), sensible tactics do not work. It is instead guerrilla war. The public manager must be willing to staff up for the fight, commit personal time and energy to the battle, sometimes sacrifice control for program implementation, and become a masterful tactician of circumvention and satisficing. The manager will have to cope by accepting the rules of the game or by evading, bending, or changing those rules, even to the point of moving all or part of the agency's operation beyond the scope of the overhead system.

Some practical rules of thumb follow.

Know the system as well or better than it knows itself.

Part of the mystique of overhead agencies lies in their complexity. All too often the rules, regulations, and procedures are designed to maintain control rather than promote effective management. A naïve manager will assume that the rules are incomprehensible; that the overhead bureaucrat is correct, not simply obscure or recalcitrant. While not the most exciting bedtime reading, the personnel manual, the contract guidelines, and the budget schedules are invaluable documents for the manager. If you are not willing to learn what the system is, and understand it, then you cannot possibly expect to cope, and you deserve everything it does to you.

Gratuitous personality conflicts are no-nos.
You've got enough problems as it is.

Good personal relationships are fundamental to the manager's dealing with the environment. While the temptation (particularly with overhead agencies) is to attribute personal motives to any adverse decision, public managers must steel themselves against such sentiments.

Overhead agencies are fickle; they can be alternately expediters and roadblocks. How well you get along with overhead staff can determine whether you get your typewriter in one week or four. Furthermore, personal antagonisms drain your energy, will sooner or later come back to haunt you, and make little sense if you are a mouse and the subject of your hostility is a tiger. There will be enough real reasons for the overhead system to lower the boom on you without your picking a personal fight with the budget director. If you really cannot stand him or her, get a subordinate you trust who can.

Organize for overhead dealings.
Pick the right staff for the job.

Overhead agency relations do not occur on their own. Left to chance, the line agency will have no room to maneuver, little probability of success in program implementation, and a limited life expectancy. Agency heads need staff to concentrate primarily or exclusively on overhead system liaison. Whether you have a staff of ten or ten thousand, a capacity to respond to overhead demands is essential.

Agency heads should take care that they have the right mix of people to work with overhead agencies. Ideal staffers will be resourceful and will refuse to be beaten by the bureaucracy. They will be do-or-die fighters who can kick, claw, and scratch with the best of them. They will be part con artist, winning with wit when the bulldog approach is unsuitable. If these staffers are longtime bureaucrats and in favor with the overhead agencies, all the better; if they used to work for the budget shop, personnel shop, or procurement agency, terrific—they will know how to circumvent better than anyone else.

If you have a candidate who looks like a bureaucrat, thinks like a street fighter, smiles like a cherub, and is married to the personnel director, sign him or her right up—that is just what the doctor ordered.

Program staff must be involved in overhead issues; it is a crucial part of their jobs.

Agency heads have to make clear to their program operators that paying attention to overhead matters is part of their responsibility; they know the substance of the programs and simply have to work as a team with the agency's fiscal and personnel types to ensure that they get what they need from the overhead system. It is a contradiction in terms to say: "I'm a program person. I'm not interested in administrative matters." In service delivery it *is* administration that matters. Nobody was ever made healthier, happier, or more independent by programs with no facilities, no staff, and no money. Caring about people means caring about the quality of services being delivered, and that quality depends in large part on how the agency and the overhead system get along.

Building positive attitudes is important to counter the negativism of the overhead system.

Public managers must spend time getting it across to staff that red tape is the enemy, that if they cannot beat it they will accomplish little, and that when the smoke clears it will be their neck on the line, not the budget analyst's. Speeches extolling the principle that "we're running the agency; they aren't" tend to help here, especially when accompanied by a lot of hard slamming of the open hand on the conference table or desk (it makes more noise that way).

You have to spend the time necessary to conquer overhead problems: (1) the soft approach.

So you think you are going to run a health department and spend all your time making people healthy? Wrong. More often than not, you as a public manager will find that more time is spent on overhead issues than on any other single problem. Fighting red tape is the only defense to being strangled by it, and as an agency head it is your responsibility to take the lead. The soft approach to agency head / overhead system relations is recommended if your credibility with the chief is not fully established (or commonly understood) or if a new administration has just arrived.

> The soft approach, which was something of a ceremony in New York City government, goes like this: The agency head goes hat in hand to the overhead, apologizing for the latest indiscretion—like bringing fourteen new attorneys on board before the positions had been established. After submitting to the inevitable dressing down from the overhead masters—in essence lying down while they ritually walk all over you—you tearfully promise to behave in the future if just this once they will bail you out and approve the jobs for these fine, upstanding, innocent young lawyers.
> Obviously you can only go to the well so often; but in the absence of the support necessary to pull off

*the hard approach it is your only option—save not
hiring the lawyers in the first place. Hair shirts are
suitable attire for the soft approach.*

You have to spend the time necessary to conquer overhead problems: (2) the hard approach.

Once you are established and have done your homework in building a solid relationship with your chief, a
more aggressive strategy may be in order. You can show
them who is boss.

The hard approach has its own conventions: First, be
prepared to squeeze the needed resources out of your
own budget or secure outside resources to achieve what
you are after—the overheads are hard put to say no if
you have the resources in hand and are just seeking
sign-off. Second, have some proof that what you are up
to will work. Evidence that you are capable of moving
quickly, staying on top of things, and producing to the
satisfaction of the chief is helpful if you want favorable
action. Third, build up some public support before you
go in. A Sunday editorial about how terrific your new
program is, or how essential the service will be to the
community's quality of life, makes it a lot easier at the
budget meeting on Monday morning. It is a sure bet to
circumvent the no or no response techniques on the
spot. Fourth, make absolutely clear that you are going
ahead no matter what the overhead bureaucrats say.
Even overhead agencies find it less painful to give in
early than to hold out for the inevitable. Bluster, in-
dignation, name dropping, and epithets are all good ac-
companiments at this stage. Finally, make sure that city
hall, the statehouse, or the White House (depending on
your level of government) knows your purpose and will
support you. The hard approach is a lot more fun as long

as you are not blowing in the wind with no chief behind you to back you up. The interesting thing about hard-line tactics with overhead agencies is that if you pull it off once, it gets easier and easier.

In short, approach the overhead agency as supplicant only until you know you are in the driver's seat. Then be direct, move ahead, do not take no for an answer, and be absolutely clear that if you have to go to the chief for resolution of the issue you have a better than fifty-fifty chance of winning.

When the soft and hard approaches fail: bypass.

Regardless of how skillful and ceremonial they become, both the soft and hard approaches to dealing with overhead agencies are based on playing by the rules. It is often the case, however, that the manager does not want the straightforward response. One of the anomalies of overhead systems is that, while there are some things that you absolutely *cannot* do, the things that you *can* do are subject to a variety of interpretations. It is a personal system where the actors know one another and talk to one another. Even though all the game playing may look senseless, it is the one thing that enables the system to sputter along at all.

There are many time-honored and legal evasions of the system which almost all agency heads practice. Their importance varies according to how intractable the overhead system is, but their utility is indisputable. On general principle, of course, one could argue that it is a shame that governments must set up alternatives and special devices to avoid their own red tape. It would seem far more sensible to change the red tape. For a variety of reasons—tradition, the difficulty of legislative change, the power of interest groups—this is easier said than done. Overhead systems are often the sacred cows that lead public managers to sacrifice control for program integrity.

Juggling is a learned skill, and it is the root of bureaucratic bypass tactics—juggling this month's payroll at the drug center to cover this month's deficit at the child care center; bringing people on board in any open job description in anticipation that "later on" you will correct the details; buying the typewriter with travel monies that you will make up with grant funds next quarter; or turning the office space for six into cubbyholes for twenty in order to get the new inspection program off the ground. Playing the bypass game can lead to administrative disorder. Caution is required. Juggling funds from one hospital to another, putting a lawyer in a janitor's job because it is the only one you have open, or using those empty offices on the fifth floor until somebody kicks you out will eventually catch up with you, and the resulting administrative chaos may take months to sort out.

As in all things, if you are going to use these tactics—and every public manager is obliged to at some time or another—at least do it well. Keep a good record of whom you put where, how they are being paid, why it was necessary, and when you did it. When the auditors come around, you will have powerful evidence of the consequences of overhead inaction and delay. Coincidentally you may also stay out of jail, and at least score a big point for your ability to get things done regardless of the obstacles.

If you can't reason and you can't bypass: escape.

So far we have discussed how the public manager can cope with the overhead system on its own turf. It is also sometimes possible, even advisable, for the public manager to escape—running some or all of the operation outside of the overhead system. Such drastic alternatives, however, have many negative as well as positive consequences.

There are two major techniques that governments use to operate outside of cumbersome overhead systems: contracting out and creating public benefit corporations or independent authorities. These two methods, along with direct administration, are the only three ways that government can provide services; and the differences among them provide important clues to when, why, and how to use them.

The advantage of direct operation of programs and services is that, once they are established, the manager (and chief executive) can maintain direct control over them. The disadvantages—the subject of this entire chapter—are the red tape, time, and difficulty involved in implementing programs in the public sector.

CONTRACTS   The method of contracting with an outside vendor has traditionally been used for capital programs, road construction, garbage collection, and other items related to public works or general services. It is, however, becoming more and more common for contracting, or purchase of care, to be used for human services delivery: prison health care, drug and alcohol treatment, foster and group home care for needy persons. Diminishing resources inevitably result in new spurts of interest in contracting out—"privatizing" in bureaucratic parlance—certain government functions.

The advantages of contracting or purchase of care are many. First, it establishes productive alliances between the public and private sectors, allowing the manager to use private resources to accomplish agency goals. Second, it reduces red tape, at least in program start-up. Third, if done properly it can lower costs— particularly if collective bargaining and civil service regulations have driven the labor costs of the public sector above those of the jurisdiction's private sector. This is often the case in human services where community-based facilities are substituted for institutional alternatives.

Disadvantages of contracting include the need to establish new, often elaborate, monitoring and accountability systems; diminished control by the public manager; and the potential for fraud through overcharging, skimming overhead costs, and other forms of fiscal irresponsibility.

A public manager who decides to provide a service through contracts should follow certain basic principles to ensure program quality and avoid fraud. First, the manager should know precisely what services are to be purchased. This sounds elementary but is a common cause of devastating failures by contracting agencies. Proposals to provide "drug treatment" are quite different from proposals to provide methadone maintenance to a specific number of addicts. While it is sometimes argued that general "requests for proposal" encourage creativity and diversity of services, more often than not they reflect a manager who really does not know what he or she wants. A better way of seeking proposals is to decide in detail what each service unit is expected to do, with what resources, and for whom. With such a model in hand the public manager need not be inflexible if better methods are suggested by the bidders, but at least there is a base-line measure for judging the alternatives' merits.

Second, the public manager should make sure that the contract is a performance contract—that a specific amount of services or deliverables is required before any payment is made. The number of times this does not occur is truly astonishing, and the results can be disastrous. If you do not specify the performance required, how can you determine whether or not the contract has been violated? Good money can follow bad simply because you have no basis to terminate the contract.

Third, contracts should be approached cooperatively, not adversarially. Remember that you are going this route to avoid all of the obstacles and red tape you encountered with your own bureaucracy; do not compound the error by establishing procedures for your service providers that would shame the most onerous overhead system. (There must be a little budget director in all of us.) While monitoring and evaluation are important, they are different from real technical assistance. The agency head should impress on subordinates that they are responsible for the success of contracted services. Public managers should reward subordinates for helping to make a contractor successful—not just for uncovering fiscal abuse or professional irresponsibility.

Fourth, you must have a reporting system and monitoring process which allows you to know what the contractor is doing. It need not be elaborate or cumbersome, but you have to be able to keep track of who is served, how, and how often. Quantitative measures of contract requirements and qualitative information on program operation are both essential for responsible contract supervision. A capacity to monitor and evaluate is useless if you are unwilling to act on the results when you have them. Providers whose contracts are continually renewed even though their performance is unacceptable set a bad example for the rest of the universe. If you will not ensure quality, you might as well just throw the money up for grabs and let service quality be damned.

Fifth, and finally, remember that contracts for human services are different from contracts for material goods. In more than one government the procedures for buying a copier are identical to the procedures for selecting a group home: request for bids, sealed proposals, "objective" review of bids, and selection of the lowest bidder. This approach is antithetical to the concept of purchase of care, which assumes a collaborative relationship between the agency and the private provider. Determining who is best to provide a service and how it should be done is not easily reduced to wholly objective criteria. If your overhead system forces you to approach human service contracting the same way you would approach construction projects, you have been had, and you should raise holy hell.

PUBLIC BENEFIT CORPORATIONS   The third alternative—public benefit corporations—is the most drastic and, from the manager's perspective, the riskiest or the most desirable or both. If the public benefit corporation's form is administrative only, not affecting program decisions and control, it can be heaven. If instead it is wholly autonomous, it can be a nightmare beyond the scope of both the overhead system and the line manager. Public corporations have some real advantages, some perceived advantages, and some real disadvantages which govern the circumstances under which they are desirable.

Among the real advantages is the flexibility this structure provides to its own management. It cuts out a good portion of the interfering players in the public manager's environment—at least on a day-to-day basis. A second real advantage is that there is often less turnover of qualified staff because the ability to provide incentives is less restricted than under civil service. Continuity of staff allows for continuity of programs and long-range planning. A third advantage is that many public corporations have the authority to raise their own revenues through bonds or taxes. This diminishes even further any dependence on the general government.

Other advantages of public corporations may be more apparent than real. It is often argued that a public corporation can have a singleness of purpose not possible in the typical government agency. This is all well and good in prosperous times, but when the fiscal crunch comes, these isolated units of public service can refuse to take their fair share, putting an even greater burden on other agencies. It is also argued that public corporations are freer from political influence than their executive branch counterparts. This too is more myth than reality. Oftentimes they may be highly politicized and (by virtue of their freedom from oversight) more, rather than less, vulnerable to political influence and control.

The disadvantages of public corporations are real and significant. First, they are not directly accountable to the public will. This is a big price to pay for service delivery and not one to be taken lightly. Second, the board of directors may create more problems than they solve in terms of competing constituencies, tendency to interfere with administration, and personal political agendas. This can be especially problematic if the authority's managers are weak or politically impotent. The very structure of these entities can contribute to dispersed authority—the board versus the management—and, as a seasoned Washington bureaucrat once observed, "I never did hear of anything with two heads living for long." Finally, the establishment of public corporations is itself an arduous and complicated process. Normally requiring special legislation, it is not an alternative that can be carried out quickly. Only in extraordinary circumstances should it be employed and then only after careful and patient planning.

Most important:
don't give up—keep fighting.

Line managers who conclude that the overhead system is impenetrable have been in government too long. They should get out or become overhead bureaucrats themselves: if you can't beat them, join them.

Overhead problems wear down even the best of managers, and you need to constantly keep up your guard against acquiescence. As long as you believe that the overhead system is conquerable, you can succeed. Organize—staff for the battle, anticipate it, and establish your ability to win early. You are the agency manager—do not let yourself be pushed around by middle-level bureaucrats. Above all else, garner your support—particularly with the chief—and have better information than they have. Put them on the defensive—it is a new experience for most overhead agencies—and then keep them on the run. You, your agency, and the public will be the better for it.

4 / Managers, Legislators, and Other Elected Officials

To be "above politics" in public management is a contradiction in terms. The public manager's world is made up of bureaucrats, citizens, and politicians; and in order to get anything done, the public manager must be adept at dealing with all three. The main politician about whom the manager is concerned is, of course, the chief executive—the boss. But there are other elected officials with whom the manager regularly contends: executive branch politicians and legislators.

Executive branch politicians are creatures of state and local government. Their powers, duties, and influence are almost as varied as the jurisdictions they serve; they include everyone from attorneys general to, quite literally, dogcatchers. From the public manager's perspective, executive branch politicians are significant because they can hurt the manager—not because of their ability to be particularly strong allies.

All public managers must deal with legislatures and legislators. Whether it is a town council or Congress, the legislature is a fundamental part of public management. Legislators pass laws which public managers turn into programs. In between are enormous pitfalls, a lot of work, and a lot of politics—they are all part of the job.

This chapter looks first at executive branch politicians—and their peculiar, often contradictory role in executive management—and then at legislators—and how the talkers affect the doers.

EXECUTIVE BRANCH POLITICIANS: "HAVING BEEN ELECTED BY THE PEOPLE . . ."

Election gives officeholders the right to introduce even the most preposterous action with this hallowed reference to the voters. While the election process is properly revered by lovers of democracy, it can be the bane of the public manager's existence—especially when it endows a political rival of the chief with the power to harass, publicly castigate, and otherwise make life miserable for the mere mortal appointed agency head.

Executive branch politicians hold constitutional positions—jobs which by stipulation of state constitutions or local charters must be filled by election. It is their being elected, more than the jobs they perform, that distinguishes executive branch politicians from their appointed executive colleagues. Being elected generally means wanting to be reelected; and even if two officials have essentially the same job, being put there by the people is fundamentally different from being put there by the chief. The motives are different, the allegiances are different, and the constraints are different.

Executive branch politicians are frequently rivals of the chief executive. They may be politically ambitious, using the constitutional office as a stepping-stone to a higher position, or they may simply be spokespersons for the rival party or a dissident faction within the chief's own party. Whatever the motive, few executive branch politicians find it expedient to tackle the chief head on. The chief's appointed agency heads, however, provide tempting surrogates. A public manager's ravaged body (and program) is always an attention grabber and excellent grist for a budding campaign challenge.

POWERS AND PROBLEMS

Executive branch politicians fall into one of three categories: those with largely ceremonial powers (secretaries of state, most lieutenant governors), those with administrative and agency responsibilities much like the appointed manager's (for example, elected agency heads in Texas, several state education commissioners, or city councilors in Portland, Oregon, who serve both legislative and executive functions), and those with investigatory, overhead or oversight functions. The latter group (which includes elected attorneys general, comptrollers, auditors, and the like) is certainly the most common and by far the most sig-nificant for the public manager.

Investigatory powers of executive branch politicians consist of preaudit review (monitoring of expenditures or decisions before the fact to ensure consistency with appropriations, regulations or authorizations), postaudit review (investigating financial and program performance *after* the fact), and legal review (oversight before, during, and after program actions to ensure legality).

Almost all public managers dislike the obstacles these investigatory powers put up to program implementation, even though the oversight often proves to be in the manager's best interest. It takes time to get contract language cleared; it is frustrating to be second-guessed on administrative decisions (especially if they had to be made in crisis situations with too few resources and too little time); and it is infuriating to contend with program delay while lawyers argue about the proper interpretation of a vaguely written regulation, statute, or court opinion.

The problems over which public managers and executive branch politicians clash are much like those that arise with respect to the overhead system (discussed in Chapter 3). In fact, many of the investigatory positions held by executive branch politicians are formally a part of the overhead system. But these disputes differ materially from conflicts with an appointed budget chief or corporation counsel; disputes with typical overhead agencies can, if necessary, be settled in the chief's office. Disputes with ambitious executive branch politicians are usually settled in public—if they are settled at all. These officials differ in an even more fundamental way from the elected chief—they have few line responsibilities and have the luxury of dabbling in the process of government without being responsible for the product.

In addition to having before- and after-the-fact arguments on administrative matters, method of service delivery, quality of services, and fiscal accountability, executive politicians and managers may clash directly on policy matters. Seats on policy-making commissions and advisory groups often give these officials an additional forum for competing with the chief, publicizing malfeasance, and otherwise scrutinizing manager actions.

The executive politician is in but not of the chief's administration. Instead of a team player, the executive politician is more like a league official—making sure the players and coaches play straight and by the league rules. The success of executive politicians is measured by the amount of wrongdoing they uncover, and to a great extent their continuation in office and their budget and staffing are dependent on public presentation of their reports, their findings, and their conclusions.

From the manager's perspective the executive branch politician can be a threat politically (depending on the nature of the relationship with the chief), programmatically (by virtue of the job's mandate for oversight and before- or after-the-fact control of decisions), and personally (by virtue of the ability to publicize criticism and hold the media's attention with allegations, investigative reports, and program evaluations). But managers should not underestimate the value they hold for these potential adversaries. Executive branch politicians cannot deliver services or programs; public managers can. This difference is a crucial one which provides the leverage and the basis for managers' strategies for dealing with the politicians.

DEALING WITH EXECUTIVE BRANCH POLITICIANS

Public managers need two separate strategies for dealing with executive branch politicians—one for the strong officials and another for the weak. In order to determine how powerful any single executive politician is, the manager should answer a series of questions: What kind of position is it? Does the executive politician have any investigative or oversight function? If there is an investigative function, how broad is the hunting license? Is it only fiscal, or fiscal and programmatic? How many staff members does the politician have? Are they accountants? social scientists? lawyers? Are their resources sufficient for a wide range of in-depth program and fiscal reviews, or are there only enough for a superficial review? Does the politician have a formal role in the overhead process? Can he or she hold up payments, stop contracts, affect hiring decisions? Can the executive politician veto administrative or executive actions? If so, when and how? Is the politician running for office against the chief? How do the politics look?

For weak executive branch politicians—those with only ceremonial or very limited powers—the manager's strategy is simple: be courteous, deferential, and responsive. You never know when the lowly executive branch politician will be elevated to governor, and besides, enemies are easy enough to come by in this business; you need not spend time manufacturing them.

If an analysis of the officials with whom you must deal suggests that they are, in fact, powerful (an investigative mandate, political aspirations, and sizable resources with skilled staff), you had better be prepared to spend a lot of time on details. Under no circumstances should a public manager knowingly circumvent the law, manipulate funds for personal advantage, or otherwise corrupt the job at hand. But reality is such that many actions, especially in a complex and controversial agency, will inadvertently run afoul of regulations, procedures, and mandates. To the extent that the manager creates an environment where staff believe the end to be more important than the means, fiscal and program accountability problems are inevitable. A manager can choose to deal with these excesses as they occur or can take the time to practice a little preventive medicine.

Given enough time and enough people, almost anybody can find something wrong in any public agency (or private organization, for that matter). For the public manager, the most important thing is to judge the likelihood that the investigative arsenal will be focused on the manager's agency; only then can the time required to cope with the politician be calculated.

When dealing with ambitious and powerful officials,

the best bet is to assume that they will hurt you if they get the chance—not because they are particularly mean or nasty but because it is their job and in their political interest to do so. Keep the following in mind when dealing with them.

Don't go out of your way to give an executive branch politician the chance to hurt you.

You are more likely to incur an executive politician's wrath if you (and your staff) do not show proper deference; if you refuse to cooperate or generally make it a policy to hold back information until it is literally pried loose; or if you go out of your way to publicly criticize or complain about the investigations under way. There are a multitude of reasons for any executive branch politician to target your agency; personality clashes and obstinacy should not be allowed to be the primary ones.

Encourage middle- and lower-level staff to make contacts with their counterparts in executive politicians' agencies.

It is amazing how much useful information travels among and between support staff in any government. It is equally incredible how quickly a personnel action can be approved if your clerk and the comptroller's clerk are cousins.

Most students of bureaucracy have noted a truth which many public officials would just as soon ignore: your staff were there before you and will likely be there after you. You should not be frightened by the informal networks which exist at government's lower levels. Instead you should use them to your advantage by creating an environment where these relationships are encouraged and given recognition.

Staff-to-staff relationships have two principal advantages: they cut down on unnecessary (time-consuming) paperwork, and they provide intelligence that can at least forewarn where the executive politician is planning to strike next. Obviously a manager needs to ensure that staff are loyal and committed to the agency's interest and mission. Once you are sure, however, interstaff networks should be utilized. Good management is the best safeguard against ambitious executive politicians, but a little advance warning never hurt either.

Run as tight a ship as possible on fiscal matters. Never, never, never play fast and loose with public funds.

The one thing the public absolutely will not stand for is fiscal incompetence or chicanery, even of the most trivial nature. The public may not be able to weigh the complexities of a given policy, but they know when money is being stolen or lost—and there is no "other side of the story." As a public manager you should make sure that you have some internal capacity to monitor and audit your own finances; if anything is going wrong, you should be the one to catch it—not the auditor or comptroller.

An attitude of fiscal integrity should be promoted and demanded at all staff levels. Discipline should be prompt and public when there has been malfeasance. Public management is complicated enough without inviting trouble on the rudiments—at least know how much money you have, where it is going, and how it is getting there.

Don't sit on anything hot for more than a second. Turn it over and cooperate.

The experience of the past decade suggests that many public officials ignore what should be a basic tenet of elected or appointed office: If you have evidence of wrongdoing, don't cover it up; report it, be investigated, and clear it up as soon as possible.

Not only is it morally offensive for public managers to ignore—or, worse, hide—wrongdoing in their agencies, it is stupid. There are altogether too many officials who have a political interest in uncovering scandal. The risk of covering up a problem is simply too great; it is inevitable that it will be uncovered, and you stand to jeopardize any good things you have done not just for the present but for your (and your chief's) future.

It is also important to remember that diligence against wrongdoing is not just an exercise for newly appointed officials. While it is more fun to uncover your predecessor's misdemeanors, it is more important to prevent your own.

Finally, in dealing with executive branch politicians, remember that it is impossible for any public manager to prevent all wrongdoing, incompetence, or fiscal irresponsibility. Executive branch politicians have the mandate and the motive to investigate your performance. Keeping clean, being cooperative, and being professional will minimize the interference of these officials but certainly will not eliminate it. Your best bet is to establish as good a personal relationship as possible with the official and his or her staff; develop a reputation for honesty and competence and hope that the politician picks on the next guy more than on you.

LEGISLATURES AND LEGISLATORS

Public managers deal with a large variety of legislative bodies: city councils, county boards, state legislatures, and the Congress. Often, depending on the manager's responsibilities, several legislatures may be involved simultaneously.

All legislative bodies, regardless of the level of government, have in common that they are a separate branch of government (not accountable to the manager's chief) and that they are more concerned with policy setting than with program implementation or operation. The legislature's relationship with the chief, and by implication the appointed manager, is likely to be one of rivalry at best and antagonism at worst.

Because the relationship between the legislature and the executive branch is crucial to the level of resources which can be commanded and the degree of administrative and political autonomy which can be exercised, it is important that public managers start with a clear understanding of the differences in perspective between elected legislators and appointed executive officials.

Legislators must stand for reelection frequently, and the most important fact of life to them will be their constituents and their own district. Legislative districts typically cover only a small portion of the area for which the chief executive is responsible and over which the manager's agency functions. In a geographical sense, legislators are highly parochial; almost anything that affects their district (or their standing in the district) is infinitely more important than anything that does not.

The special interests of the district will determine the special interests of the legislator and will shape the perspective from which the legislator views the manager, the manager's agency, and the manager's requests. Often these interests transcend district lines—rural legislators are interested in rural problems whether immediate to home or not—but will still color the legislator's approach to executive policy matters.

Legislators typically have little or no interest in the day-to-day details of program implementation, which of course is the primary concern of the public manager. There are two basic reasons for this lack of concern.

First, legislators generally do not have public management backgrounds. The overwhelming majority are lawyers, and lawyering is a talking rather than a doing profession. Law is an excellent background for writing legislation but not necessarily for writing legislation that can be easily translated from paper to an operating program.

Second, the legislator has little political incentive to care about implementation. The legislator makes a name—and increases reelection prospects—by passing legislation and investigating the conduct of others, not by being accountable for program implementation. If a program turns out to be a fiasco, the blame can be squarely placed on the public manager who was not "good enough" or did not "know enough" to implement the legislation properly. If, on the other hand, a program turns out to be a roaring success, the legislator can claim the lion's share of the credit, without the headaches of recruiting staff, developing budgets, or suffering endless hours of frustration at the hands of the overhead system, interest groups, and unsatisfied clients.

It is important for the public manager to remember that measures of legislative success are considerably different from measures of management success and that this creates a gulf over which communication and understanding can become especially strained.

Legislators and managers

Legislators can be expected to want certain things from a public manager. On a personal level legislators want respect—and its companion, access to the manager whenever and wherever the legislator feels necessary. No one gets elected to public office without a sizable ego; and deference, while not always deserved, is a wise policy. Legislators will also want services for constituents in their districts and, more often than not, special favors for special interests in their districts.

The legislator is likely to be a political rival of the chief, if not as a potential candidate, then at least in the sense of wanting to take credit for the good and to shift blame for the bad to another branch of government. If the legislator is a political ally of the chief and the chief is powerful, this rivalry can be tempered just by sharing the credit. If they are active opponents, however, the rivalry will be more serious. Legislators want publicity, the lifeblood of political survival. As a result, they will want to use public managers as targets for publicity, both in the sense of publicizing grants, programs, or services obtained for constituents and in the investigative sense—uncovering poor performance or malfeasance in the manager's agency.

The ability of the legislature and of individual legislators to hurt the public manager will depend on the scope of explicit powers (granted by federal, state, or local constitutions and charters), the resources available, the political circumstances during any given legislative session, and the personalities of the individual legislators.

The key variable is the resources available to the legislature to carry out its powers. Where the legislative staff is large and sophisticated, the manager and the manager's programs can come under much closer scrutiny than where the staff is small and ineffectual. The same holds true for individual legislative staffs— powerful legislators command powerful resources and are in a much better position to concentrate on specific problems or programs than are their less affluent colleagues.

Legislators are typically involved with a wide range of issues and causes, and it is impossible for them to be expert on all matters. Therefore, in addition to being political fodder, the manager must contend with the lack of education on the legislator's part about the intricacies of the manager's agency, the constraints facing the manager, and the implications of certain legislative decisions for administrative and program performance. Legislators are almost always skeptical of managers' motives and of performance data provided by managers; this can be especially frustrating to managers if the legislator has limited knowledge of the area at issue.

Managers and legislators: intersections

The major points where managers and legislators intersect are on budget, oversight and, not surprisingly, legislation.

The role of the legislature in budget making is fairly similar across levels of government. In most cases the legislature responds to requests prepared by the executive branch. The degree of sophistication of the budget review and the power of the legislature with respect to budget items again depend on the statutory powers and the quality of the staff available to assist in exercising those powers.

The budget process produces predictable conflicts between public managers and legislators. The size of the budget and the number of staff are common fighting grounds. The manager normally wants more than the legislature is willing to provide. The chief executive gets reelected by doing things, and "things" cost money. Legislators, on the other hand, rarely get plaudits for program implementation, but they get good press for holding the line and curbing the spendthrift tendencies of cushy bureaucrats. Psychological factors are at work as well: few people like to be seen as rubber stamps, and

the inescapable fact that legislatures must always respond to the chief's proposals provides keen incentive
for trying to change some of the chief's priorities—it
would almost be "unmanly" not to do so.

> *While I, like most New Yorkers, viewed the City
> Council as a funny, ineffective place, unlike most
> New Yorkers, I could be hurt by it. Therefore, my
> general strategy was to deal politely and respon-
> sively with the Council, giving them little cause to be
> mad at me personally, and to minimize the amount
> of my time and my staff's in dealing with them.*
> *Several kinds of situations would bring one into
> contact with the City Council.*
> *One was that at least once a year I would have to
> present myself before the Council to defend my
> budget. These were marvelous sessions. After a
> few probing questions into the heart of our one-
> billion-dollar agency's mission, like "How come you
> have ten drivers in the Health Department instead
> of eight?" they would then permit questions from
> whichever of their few colleagues had been able to
> drag themselves to the session. Whereupon, believe
> it or not, the questions would go downhill. They
> would go downhill in two directions—they were
> either incredibly picayune or incredibly cosmic.*

Naturally legislators are concerned about the amount
of money and resources being directed toward their
district and constituents. In many instances decisions
on substantive matters will depend on how much a particular district can expect to benefit; this is especially
true in cases where benefits to one group must come at
the expense of benefits to another.

Another predictable area of conflict involves legisla-
tively imposed limits on the executive's ability to imple-

ment the budget. Most legislatures do not have line-by-line, penny-by-penny authority, but even so their involvement and restrictions can be onerous. This is particularly true when the chief executive and the legislature (or individual legislator) are at odds over a specific program or policy; virtually all appropriations bills—regardless of level of government—contain some mandated programs or policies. Reorganization by appropriation is a popular game in many council chambers, statehouses, and congressional committees.

While these types of legislative intervention may frustrate the manager, they can have positive consequences as well. The manager may be better off, especially when a project or program the manager supports has been opposed by the chief but restored by the legislature. The manager gets a program he or she might otherwise not have. However, it comes at the price of extraordinarily decreased flexibility. The legislature has said not only what must be done but how it must be done, and it is necessary to go back to the legislature for any changes, regardless of detail. Managers should resist the temptation to habitually seek legislative restoration of programs, resources, or policies disapproved by the chief executive. Such a pattern is quickly recognized in the chief's office and is unlikely to bring rewards.

Legislators and public managers are certain to conflict over policy or lawmaking initiatives from either side. Legislators' often limited understanding of the agency's mission and constraints may make this conflict particularly taxing. Well-staffed legislative committees and offices may feel confident that they have as much or more expertise in a given area than the agency itself and may want to dictate to agency managers both general and specific policies and programs. Poorly prepared or understaffed aides, on the other hand, may produce ill-conceived legislation in the name of reform and quick fixes. In either case, legislative liaison is a delicate balancing act which places the manager in the middle between the chief and legislators seeking to attack or at least intervene in the chief's and the manager's agenda.

Legislators and public managers will inevitably interact on jobs. While the extent of direct legislative authority over personnel actions varies from state to state and city to city, all legislators are concerned with the public payroll and with ensuring that people they favor get jobs and people they dislike are rebuffed.

Finally, and most importantly, the legislator and the public manager will conflict over constituent services. It is impossible for any public agency to be all things to all people, and invariably someone's constituent ends up on the short end of the stick.

Manager/legislator interaction about constituents occurs on two levels. At one level the public manager should expect the legislator to fight for the collective good of constituents—which translates simply into getting as much government spending as possible into the district. At another level legislators are vitally concerned about what happens to the complaints of individual constituents. The constituent is typically complaining about some public service that was not properly delivered. Such complaints are taken very seriously. Legislators—or at least their staffs—spend a great deal of time on "casework." This concern leads many managers to conclude that legislators do little but ask, ask, ask about the complaints of their constituents.

As with virtually all aspects of public management, negatives can be turned to positives with a little creativity and work on the manager's part. Legislators are responsive to complaints but also to compliments; constituent congratulations on good service delivery can be as helpful as constituent complaints are harmful.

And again, legislators cannot deliver services—only managers can; so the relationship is, by definition, symbiotic.

Coping with legislators is often a time-consuming aspect of a public manager's work. Making the task somewhat more palatable and productive is the subject of the next section.

LEGISLATIVE RELATIONS: THE VIEW FROM THE MANAGER'S CORNER

The public manager must conduct all legislative relations with an awareness of the potential for good as well as bad. The legislature often controls the level of resources available to the manager and thus is, inescapably, critical to the public manager's performance. Public managers deal with individual legislators, not with legislatures. The diversity of legislators' personalities, interests, and expertise requires a similarly diverse strategy for legislative relations. Some legislators will require considerably more time and attention from the manager than will others.

Be selective.

A handful of key legislators will be very important to the manager: the members, particularly senior majority members, of the agency's authorizing and funding committees. On the authorizing committees the manager is likely to find legislators who, over years of incumbency, have acquired considerable expertise in the field and from whom other members take their cues. It is obviously unwise to offend such legislators. The public manager who decides to close an important installation—a hospital or military base, for example—in one of these members' districts had better be in a very strong position. Failing that, the manager had better start running off copies of his or her résumé.

Establish good personal relations.

Virtually all public managers in governments with influential legislatures would agree that it is useful to establish close and cordial relationships with key legislators at least. Informal relationships facilitate formal transactions, and lawmaking is fundamentally a personal, interactive affair. Getting to know significant legislators and their staffs and keeping legislators personally informed (if not personally involved) in the manager's program are crucial both to the manager's image and to the manager's credibility. There is often hell to pay if this personal dimension is ignored; sooner or later details of agency goals, positions, and activities will become known to legislators. Delivering the message personally and cordially is always best—especially when the problems or activities are controversial.

Legislators are their staff.
Remember that and take time to work on it.

Almost equal in importance to the public manager's personal relationship with the legislator is the manager's relationship to legislative staff.

Dealings on a staff level (between the manager and legislative staffs and between the manager's subordinates and staff) are much more common than one-to-one dealings with legislators. Public managers should be sure that they and their subordinates are well versed in the care and feeding of legislative assistants. Frequent communication, assistance when possible, cooperation, and general respect for the significance of the legislative staff role will help. These folks rarely get the glory and attention commanded by their elected bosses, and too often their critical role in legislative decision making is overlooked or deemed secondary because it appears secondary. Few successful public managers make this mistake.

Legislative staffs are overworked; collaboration accrues to their benefit as well as yours.

Where personal or committee staffs are small, staff resources are likely to be stretched far beyond their means. When policy issues which directly affect the manager and the agency's programs are under consideration, the manager should take the initiative to seek collaboration with legislative staff. The public manager should offer assistance on legislative homework—briefing papers, backup materials for legislative histories, comparative analyses of options, and similar staff materials. While such proffers of assistance may initially be viewed with skepticism, they will generally be appreciated and will aid in ensuring that legislative discussions are at least framed in terms favorable to the manager.

Handle constituent requests promptly and courteously, even when the answer is no.

Constituents complaining about government services expect neither tact nor promptness from the offending agency. They deserve and should receive both. Public managers should take special care to handle constituent requests quickly and tactfully. When a yes is possible, it should be made expeditiously and the legislator and staff informed that the issue has been resolved. When a no is necessary, the constituent and the legislator should get a personal explanation from the manager (or someone senior enough to indicate that the agency is taking the problem seriously), detailing the reasons why the service cannot be provided or the problem resolved in the manner requested. Taking the time to explain your position and justify your action eases the negative response; just be sure that you are on firm ground and have legitimate reasons for denial.

Legislative investigations are war; you have to organize your defense.

This is an area where public managers and legislators are really adversaries. While oversight is a continuing process, investigation is a one-shot event. An investigation frequently involves public hearings which get into the newspapers and on the air. Investigations with their media attraction are likely to be politically rather than substantively oriented. All this spells trouble for the public manager.

My preparations for a City Council investigation were much different from those I made for routine oversight or budget review. Investigation was war. There were normally plenty of media around with mouths watering for what they love best—the controversial and the bitter. Usually, the members conducting the investigation were loaded for bear and intent on being "stars" in front of the media. The way they do this is to make you look bad.

In this kind of event, I prepared meticulously and knew what I was going to say. If it was a bad situation, I took the line that I knew it was bad, and then I would go on to show what I was doing about it. I tried to be as tough and nondefensive as I could. But as well as I thought I had done and as much as I

*may have prepared, I never once enjoyed reading
any newspaper the next morning. The story headlines and lead paragraph would almost always
favor the attacker, as in "Lag in Medical Care in
Jails, [my job] Hit by [Councilman Carter] Burden."*

The only defenses against legislative interrogation
are good management and meticulous preparation.
Even with the best track record and most careful staff
work, the public manager is unlikely to come out of these
episodes looking better than when he or she went in. Expectations that you can prove to a politically motivated
investigative body that your motives, actions, and
policies on a controversial issue merit praise, not blame,
are simply naïve.

Good staff relationships can help make legislative
grilling more civil, but the manager should expect things
to get ugly and should remember that the legislator invariably maintains the upper hand.

Public managers should be careful not to give
legislators gratuitous reasons to go after their heads.
Personal dislike, poor treatment of legislators' constituents, and public mockery of legislators' positions
are usually unnecessary and counterproductive.

Sooner or later each public manager's turn will come
up for legislative inquisition. While you cannot quite sit
back and enjoy it, you can minimize the anguish by being
thorough, well organized, and well prepared. At least
the war may be held to a few skirmishes.

Always be careful not to compromise
the chief executive in the delicate game
of legislative relations.

The public manager's obligation is first and foremost
to the chief executive. If ideological, political, or

personal reasons render you unable to maintain the obligation, you should not be working in that job.

Not compromising the chief in the manager's legislative dealings is particularly tough during political campaigns or on issues where the legislature's posture is more closely aligned with the manager's opinion than is the chief's. Currying favor with legislators at the expense of the chief's stature, authority, or political position may work in the short run or where the chief's power is extraordinarily weak and limited. In general, however, this is a dangerous strategy and likely to undermine the agency manager personally and the agency's programs and policies.

Cooperate, don't capitulate.
In the end we're all in it together.

Good information, professionalism, and a willingness to propose reasonable alternatives to meet legislative goals will all aid immeasurably in public managers' relationships with legislators.

If new laws are inevitable—and this is, after all, the business of these bodies—it is better for the public manager to work with the legislature to make them as palatable (and manageable) as possible. A "hands off" or "don't blame me" approach helps no one and leaves the manager vulnerable to take full blame when the poor legislation backfires.

Checks and balances mean just that, and the inevitable tension between executive and legislative officials is simply a natural consequence of our institutions of government. Public managers must mediate the differences between elected executives and elected representatives and do their best to build workable programs and services from rhetoric. The task is not enviable but it is inescapable. Learning to live with legislatures is a fact of life for all public managers. You can choose to make it tolerable or catastrophic. But remember that few people are made healthier or safer, or environments cleaner, or buses more prompt, by agencies with too few resources, too little power, and too restrictive legislative control. If you are serious about public management, you will be serious about legislative relations.

5 / Managers, Communities, Special Interests

They're everywhere—special interests, neighborhood associations, single-issue lobbies, unions, business organizations, professional associations: pressure groups. They have in common a desire to influence government decisions; to get policies, programs, and services done their way. Their importance to the public manager will vary according to the capability of the group itself and according to the nature of the agency for which the manager is responsible. Though pressure groups are more important in some situations than in others, few public managers who want to stay public managers can ignore them with impunity.

Politics—in the sense of people outside of government seeking to influence government's actions—occurs every day of the year, and pressure groups are the vehicle for much of that process. They are also the main channel through which the public manager meets the public—the manager's ultimate employer.

People organize to get jobs or money; people organize to hold government accountable for specific policies, programs, and services; people organize to make demands and to make them stick. Power—most often in the form of the ability to deliver votes—gathers in these organizations.

Elected officials meet their makers—the public— most directly on election day when votes provide the absolute unambiguous measure of their success. For public managers it is not so straightforward. They must constantly assess whether the public—in the form of pressure groups—is with them or against them, and invariably they will find some of both. Like Candid Camera, pressure groups are likely to turn up when they are least expected. Unlike Candid Camera, they rarely say "just kidding, it was all in fun" when the encounter is over. For the public manager on the receiving end the toll can be enormous, both personally and professionally.

The extent of pressure-group influence on the day-to-day operations of an agency depends on the nature of the agency itself. Agencies that contract for goods and services are subject to demands for jobs, money, and contracts.

Regulatory agencies are also subject to groups with an economic interest in the agencies' decisions—the industries being regulated, the unions representing workers in the industries, and the professional groups being licensed. Regulatory agencies are being confronted increasingly with the type of pressure group that has long been familiar to direct services agencies: the popular pressure group. This has occurred in large part as a result of the consumer movement and public concern about regulatory integrity.

Popular pressure groups include community organizations, good-government groups and single-issue groups. While the distinction between economic and popular interests is not absolute, this chapter will focus primarily on the popular groups that most directly affect the manager responsible for providing public services.

Being able to distinguish among popular pressure groups, anticipating when, how, and where each is likely to materialize, and knowing which pressure group situations require personal attention and which do not are essential skills for the public manager's portfolio. Almost everyone with whom the manager deals has a cause. The public manager must be able to gauge the depth of emotion behind a cause and the range of its popular appeal. The manager must also understand pressure group strategies and anticipate them. These functions are as much a part of the public manager's job as the annual budget.

CLASHING WITH CONSTITUENTS: WHEN WILL IT HAPPEN?

For other actors in the public manager's environment, we have been able to predict specific circumstances when intersection will occur and whether or not that intersection is likely to produce conflict or accord.

From the public manager's point of view, the only thing predictable about pressure groups is that someone somewhere has an interest in every side of every government decision. If the people with an interest find the people who make the decision—and they always do—then the pressure group process is in motion. Whether it is jobs, money, programs, or policies, advocates and opponents will find you, make their case, and monitor your performance. Even the most innocuous regulation can incur the wrath of somebody; and if those "somebodies" find one another and then find you, you will know what public management is all about.

For the manager of direct services the most important thing about pressure group relations is anticipation—assessing the lay of the land; using your head about which person or group is likely to be concerned about a decision, why and when; and preparing to provide a response and defend it under pressure.

If your services are neighborhood-based, it is inevitable that community groups will be part of your daily routine. If you deal in controversial areas—for example, abortion reform or equal employment opportunity—you know that single-issue groups will be an integral part of your job. If you have responsibility for things that affect people's livelihood—jobs, money regulation, licenses—you know that unions, professional organizations, and economic interests will be hot on your heels.

For any service it is relatively easy to predict the game card: groups representing potential recipients, groups representing people who have been excluded from participation, groups upset because you are doing too little, groups upset because you are doing too much, and groups upset that you are doing anything at all. There will even be groups upset just to be upset; like the gadflies at stockholders meetings, their "one share of stock" is the fact that they live in the city or state and their main recreation is berating bureaucrats and politicians.

Thinking through the scenario and listing all the likely players is the first step in coping with pressure groups. As you go along you can complete the actual casting— identifying who represents which predictable interest and why. Chances are that such anticipation will prevent surprise endings or an unexpected villain turning up in the last act to steal the show. If, at the end of your tenure, the cast is not complete—no angry neighborhood groups even though you run halfway houses; no pro-life assault even though you are responsible for the city's abortion clinics—you were either lucky, asleep, a genius, or in office for less than a month.

UNDER PRESSURE:
COPING WITH THE SPECIAL INTERESTS

"Between a rock and a hard place" is an oft-repeated expression in the public sector. And in no other part of the manager's world are you more likely to be damned if you do and damned if you don't than in dealing with competing interest groups. If you side with one group, their rivals will have your head; if you placate all, you will undermine your ability to do anything; if you placate none, you will be in constant confrontation, with little time to do your job.

So where should the line be drawn? What constitutes the balance between pragmatism and integrity, politics and program merits? How can you contend with pressure groups without offending your boss, undermining your mission, or alienating one group after another whose support is crucial to your program? The answer, based on agonizing experience, seems pretty basic: be honest, stay alert, and stay objective.

Pressure groups are notorious for giving public managers headaches, heartburn, and indigestion. But here are some basic characteristics of these groups and a few bromides that should provide some relief.

COMMUNITY GROUPS:
GRASS ROOTS ADVOCACY

Every jurisdiction has its community groups: neighborhood associations, civic groups, block clubs, church committees, and resident activists. The leaders and members of these groups are everyday players in the public manager's world; their organizations form an essential part of politics' grass roots. When well established and carefully organized, these groups can wield tremendous influence over government decisions affecting their constituents. When newly formed and poorly organized, they can be volatile and unpredictable—alternately allies and adversaries.

For the public manager, the relationship with community groups is complex. Community groups can be, at one and the same time, consumers of the manager's programs, monitors of government performance, informed advocates with legitimate grievances, and uninformed obstacles to program implementation.

Wherever government services are provided or promised, community groups will form, be vocal, and be demanding. The manager learns quickly that they are a daily factor in policy considerations, political judgments, resource allocation, and program delivery.

> One of the most striking things about New York City is the number of New Yorkers who really care. Obviously, in a democracy, this is not only a philosophical good but a necessary pressure on government. However, I must confess that as a public servant besieged by a screaming, caring community group, I occasionally wished they cared less; I longed for that great apathetic public which the pollsters and political scientists sometimes tell us still exists. Indeed it may, but not in New York City; and I suspect it is a vanishing species all across the United States.

> There are some good reasons why New Yorkers seem to care more. New Yorkers are organized people. New York City with seven million inhabitants is an awfully big hometown. New Yorkers make it smaller by organizing themselves around neighborhoods, politics, local issues, interests, even around city blocks, to make the landscape smaller in scale and give themselves a sense of home.

Moreover, the real caring in New York City is heightened by the fact that in New York City it is respectable to care out loud. In other parts of the country, it may be de rigueur to care quietly and deeply; write letters to congressmen; debate gently with high officials, and ask penetrating but polite questions.

Not so in New York. When New Yorkers care, they let you know about it. They sit in on you, shout at you, picket you, blast you in the press, turn politicians against you, and in general use every device or lever at their disposal. In Washington, an enemy might sneak around for weeks, wait for an opportunity, and then stab you in the back. In New York, your enemies are more likely to march up resolutely, look you in the eye, and stab you in the chest—preferably with media, political rivals, and important constituents present.

Community groups have particular characteristics which distinguish them from other types of pressure groups.

Community groups do not consider themselves part of the establishment; in fact, many of their grievances have to do with being kept out of it. What they want more than anything else is the power to influence. They want a piece of the action, they want some control, and they want some recognition. Once they become part of the establishment, community activists often realize that it looks quite different from the enemies' vantage; but until then they will be vocal, they will criticize, and they will demand more, better and faster, from the government.

Along with influence, community groups want jobs. They want jobs that give them power. They want their people to control agencies of government because they do not believe that they can be adequately represented otherwise. And they want jobs for their constituents in institutions and programs serving their area.

Community groups organize around a particular geographic area or local institution. Whether representing a neighborhood, an institution, or a particular neighborhood issue—health care, land use, education—the community group has a life of its own and does not dissolve once the specific problem or issue is resolved. This continuity gives them considerable power, as they can easily translate organizational into political power. Public managers and elected officials know this all too well.

Community groups have a leader, active members, and a constituency. Their leaders are often motivated by a desire for personal prestige and recognition, as these are among the few compensations for the work. These are not necessarily negative attributes, but they sometimes have unfortunate consequences. A community leader whose power is slipping might do anything to retain it—including things that are emotional, irrational, or just plain dumb. Actions designed to get attention or get one's name in the press are often employed at the public manager's expense, and the ruckus they create takes considerable time and effort to straighten out.

Active members mean an ability to mobilize quickly and produce bodies to work for the cause. Identifiable constituencies—whether they are active in leading the effort or passive in supporting the leaders—are the source of community group power. Failure to understand that holding a constituency means being able to deliver on their demands will topple a local leader in short order. There is always an opportunistic rival ready to take over when the leader fumbles.

Community groups are, by definition, parochial. Their concerns are localized and are bound to be more narrow than the concerns of the chief or public manager.

While individual members may have a real interest in, say, city or statewide health care, the bottom line is whether the hospital in their neighborhood stays open—not the one fifty miles away.

Community groups are politically well connected. They have tight links to their city council, county board, statehouse, and congressional representatives. It is not by coincidence that community groups are more closely identified with legislative than with executive officials. The legislator depends wholly or primarily on the local area for election, while the mayor or the governor usually has a larger jurisdiction and the ability to balance one community group against another. The symbiotic relationship between community groups and legislative officials can work to the advantage of a public manager, as few legislators will oppose a manager who has won the trust and following of the local groups.

In addition to their political power, community groups have two other important sources of influence: their ideology and public officials' fear of confrontation.

Community groups represent "the people" in a way that self-interested politicians and bureaucrats cannot claim to. This ideology gives community group leaders a distinct advantage over the planner and public manager.

No public official solicits or encourages confrontation—at least not in the form of demonstrations, sit-ins, and picket lines. But the use of confrontation tactics and implied and real threats of violence is frequently associated with community organizations. These tactics involve unscheduled interruptions in the routine of government; for managers of large and controversial agencies, they may become a way of life.

It is difficult to convey the emotional and profes-sional pressures that confrontation tactics place on public managers. Examples are countless: ten constituents barging into your office to protest a rumored program cutback; fifteen more in your outer office ready to tear you limb from limb for having too few doctors in their local clinic; a drug program administrator barricaded in an office by irate addicts; or a hundred cheerless demonstrators on your building steps at the crack of dawn hurling epithets.

The frequency of these encounters does not lessen their unpleasantness, and while the reliance on these forms of protest may be decreasing as community groups become more politically sophisticated and powerful, their potential use remains a problem for many administrators.

These kinds of confrontations, and in fact many more routine manager / community group exchanges, develop their own sort of protocol. In New York City in the late sixties and early seventies they became a sort of ritual which went something like this:

First the group would arrive—by appointment or, more commonly, unannounced. The leader would open by delivering a vivid and emotional denunciation of the manager, insinuating all manner of crimes against humanity (like wanting to close down a neighborhood hospital, or enslave all heroin addicts with methadone).

After the initial speech the torch was passed on to successive group members, each of whom repeated and embellished the charges and complaints. Any public administrator who expected to be treated with civility or deference during this stage of the ceremony was sorely mistaken; you wouldn't want your mother to hear what these good citizens thought of her baby boy or girl.

All the while the other members of the entourage would keep busy—intermittently injecting obscenities, pounding the table to emphasize the speaker's point, or wandering around the office looking at papers and generally making it clear that the manager was no hotshot in the group's eyes, no matter how lofty the title or major the responsibility.

Finally the group would issue their demands—or more often their ultimatums. If you waited patiently enough, you would eventually get your chance to speak. As we shall see later, the manager's response at this stage of the ritual has consequences beyond the immediate encounter and sets the tone for future community group relations—not just with the current guests but with other organizations as well.

The really frustrating thing about these encounters—given all the other obstacles thrown up in the face of good public management—is that community groups are usually right or at least partially right in their complaints.

Why do community groups tend to be generally right on the merits? Unlike most other groups that may affect health care (or any other government service)—such as unions, overhead agencies, press—which are motivated primarily by things other than making people healthy (for example, jobs, saving money, selling newspapers), a community group involved in health is primarily motivated by a desire to make people healthy. To be sure, some participants in the community group may have other agendas, but these people can be brought into line by the rest of the group, which will be interested in making people healthy.

Another way of putting it: A hospital union, for example, can be faced with a legitimate conflict between making people healthy and some other objective like striking a hospital (and causing people to be unhealthy) for higher wages.

Community groups do not have—to the same extent—these "legitimate" conflicts. They are for the people and therefore the merits. It gives them great strength and in my view a very high batting average for being right on the issues. The times when they tend to be wrong are those times when "illegitimate" conflicts become apparent—where making people healthy goes at cross purposes with a particular leader's agenda.

As usual, the incentive system is key. If you are a union leader, you become big in your field if you get wage increases for your membership. If you are a publisher, you become respected if you sell newspapers. If you are a community leader, to be successful you have to deliver; and the only things you can deliver are jobs and—through pressure—better services.

Nothing in government works so well or so fairly as it might, and most things are sadly very far from the mark. On bad days, with a succession of irate citizens on your doorstep, this may seem particularly true of your own agency. But community groups represent government's consumers, and they know, see, and suspect things that even the best manager may miss. They provide a mirror on government's performance and for this reason are important to the manager who wants to know how programs are doing, whom they are reaching, and how they could be made better.

While community group tactics may be unpleasant,

offensive, or just plain unnerving, it is critical for the public manager to remain objective about the merits of the complaints. Have they got a point? Why do they feel this way? What can I do about it? These are the questions that should be on the manager's mind in any community group encounter.

Many public managers see community groups (and their single-issue and do-gooder cousins) as merely a nuisance, about as welcome as brush fires in Los Angeles or locusts in Kansas. Sometimes community groups can behave like perfectly civil adults. They schedule appointments, make their case on the merits, listen to your side, and accept a reasonable compromise. But not often. More common is the ritual described earlier—confrontation, abuse, and impossible demands. It is this behavior that has led many managers (incorrectly) to a simple approach to community group relations: ignore them.

While the temptation to kick out rowdy demonstrators or have a quiet dinner instead of attending one more neighborhood meeting is understandable, it is not the approach recommended here. Whether you like it or not, in the long run you need community groups much more than they need you.

You need them politically because there are no chiefs who want their appointees dubbed anti-community— read anti-constituent, anti-voter.

You need them professionally because many of your services depend on the goodwill and cooperation of the "folks down there." It is a lot easier for a community group to stop that new drug clinic in their neighborhood than for you to get it open. Denying this premise is a little like standing in the rain with no umbrella on the theory that you do not want it to be raining and therefore you will not get wet.

And you need them personally. You have enough

problems without having to put up with constant abuse and harassment from irate and antagonistic citizens. Ignoring community groups out of spite or because of one or two bad encounters will only drain your energy and harden the opposition. And the reputation as anti-community will follow you no matter how repentant you become.

The most important reason why public managers should not simply ignore community groups has been mentioned before but deserves emphasis: community groups represent your consumers, and they are often right, or at least partly right, in their complaints. If you cannot accept this proposition, you ought to be in another business.

Community groups may be parochial, dissident, unreasonable, and arbitrary, but they do provide a perspective on your agency, your performance, and your programs. If they are wrong, as a public official you have an obligation to try to set the record straight. If they are right, you have an obligation to try to do something about it. Neither objective is met by a policy of hear no evil, see no evil, speak no evil.

Here are some of the basics.

Find the strong leaders.
Your life will be easier.

From the public administrator's point of view, it is far better to deal with a community leader who has strong backing and support than with a weak and ineffectual one. The leader may be tougher to deal with as a result, but at least he or she can afford to behave responsibly. It is the weak leaders and the would-be leaders who present problems. They are generally far less interested in the merits of a particular case than in how they look to their constituents. Not unlike politicians, for that matter. But that doesn't make it right in either case.

Don't fight one on one.
Get competing interests together
and let them work on each other.

One of the most difficult problems with community groups is their parochialism. The public manager who deals with each competing group one at a time inevitably becomes the "bad guy" to all. One way to break down parochialism is to build up awareness and knowledge of each other's problems. Facilitate direct communication between competing neighborhoods, between consumers and providers, or among rival block clubs. Eventually time and prolonged association will force compromise, or at least generate a better appreciation of the opposition's demands and what you as the manager are up against when it comes to tough choices. Task forces, committees, or other vehicles used to bring competing interests together will work only with good staffing. You should try to provide staff who know better than to play one group off against another; staff who can remain objective and command the respect of all factions; and staff who represent you and your agenda well.

Don't fight fire with fire;
it's tempting, but you'll get burned.

During ritual confrontations with community groups, it is awfully tempting to shout back, debate, and stomp harder than they do—good for the ego but not constructive. More often than not you will be shouted down, and your credibility and professionalism will be permanently injured. They will know they can goad you, and the pressure will increase, not abate.

Unless it is absolutely impossible, see demonstrators right away; do not let them cool their heels, build up tension, or become uncomfortable. Above all else, do not be condescending; turning demonstrators over to low-level staff or otherwise trying to pacify them with anything short of personal intervention will only make matters worse. It is better to see them and get it over with than to drag the confrontation on beyond everyone's tolerance.

During the attack phase of confrontations—when they state their case—keep quiet. Stay calm (even while you fight the pain of your incipient ulcer) and look intent and concerned (not cocky). You will eventually have your day in court, and it will be a whole lot easier if you have avoided being baited by the group's tactics.

If you can head off the demonstration, do it— but at least agree on the rules of the game.

If you have advance warning of a confrontation or demonstration (and you are much more likely to if your community relations are good), contact the leaders personally and try to reach a compromise. If they are right and you can do something, do it, and provide evidence of your commitment. If they are wrong but you cannot convince them, or if they need to go ahead with the demonstration for their own image, at least get the ground rules straight. Find out how many are involved, when and where the demonstration will occur, and how long it will last. Agree on the setting, the access to the facility, and the circumstances under which police will be called in.

Do not display force for its own sake. Keep police informed, but do not greet the demonstrators looking like an armed camp. Of course you will need to respond to violence, but take care not to escalate the tension.

Your best defense is facts; learn to love data.

Generally speaking, community groups do not have the capacity or resources to analyze their problems or the implications of their proposals and demands. Their objectives can often be quite narrow and symbolic. For example, they may consider a battle won by the placement of an ally in a hospital administrator's job. Of course, such a symbol does not ensure adequate performance. Community groups must be made to realize this; they must gain the information and skills to really understand local service problems and to evaluate the new administrator's performance on objective grounds. The public manager must maintain a steady flow into the community of easily understood information. This will help lessen the number of decisions based solely on political motives. The only adequate defense is facts—information on the quantity, quality, and nature of the services provided; comparisons of neighborhoods across the city, throughout the state, or in other cities; and forecasts of the impact of alternatives—the group's, yours, and others. These kinds of data cannot be pulled out of a hat; and haphazard or poorly reasoned information may be worse than none. It takes analysis, planning, and money to know what your programs are doing, what might be expected if they were changed, and how they affect a particular block in a particular neighborhood.

Too often this analytic capacity is seen as a luxury, which hard-pressed service providers can ill afford. This is partly because analysis can only be responsive to your needs and interests if you get involved. If you do not make clear what you want, why you want it, and how you want to use it, you are bound to get products that seem incomprehensible to you (and the community group) and that hardly justify the expense. In this case the solution is not to stop doing analyses but rather to do them differently—and better.

If you anticipate the needs of your agency, think through what you want to know about your programs and services, and participate in the design of analysis and supervision of your analysts, good information will result and can be your most powerful tool.

Analysis on its own will not be the whole answer. Managers must stay well attuned to the personal and political dynamics of the groups with whom they deal. But good decisions cannot be made without good information. And if it helps you get along with community groups as well, all the better.

Be honest, straightforward, and courteous.

Those scouting creeds were not kidding. Community groups have been dealing with public officials long enough to spot a lie, evasion, or waffle a mile away. They expect you to be less than candid, to promise things you cannot deliver, to say anything to get them out of your way, or to just plain lie to save your own neck. Furthermore, they want to force you to see it their way; to intimidate you, if necessary, into deciding in their favor. If you agree with them it's no problem, but if you know that what they ask is wrong, you simply cannot give in. To make a bad decision just to appease a pressure group in the heat of the moment is not only wrong, it is stupid. When the ceiling caves in as a result of what you knew was a problem all along, the community groups will not be there to back you up.

No matter how unpleasant it is at the time, if you cannot or will not go along with a group's demands, be forthright. If you have not made up your mind, say that too, and be candid about when and how a final decision will be made. You may not enjoy it at the time, but you will be the better for it later on.

Managers who take community concerns seriously, do what they can when they can, and base their arguments on the merits will eventually develop good relationships with community groups. At least the confrontations will get easier, the animosity less intense, and the limits of authority—yours and theirs—better understood. The more sophisticated and influential the community group, the less reason they will have to be nasty to you. The more powerful as a group these organizations become, the fewer options you will have.

GOOD-GOVERNMENT GROUPS: PROCESS WATCHERS, POLICY TALKERS

While some community groups have real political power and some have the power to agitate, good-government groups have only the power to comment and suggest.

Good-government group members include men and women who are diversified in age, race, and income. What they have in common is concern about the process of government (sometimes more than the outcome) and membership in the establishment; they are generally comfortable, successful, and active in their communities. They want to influence "policy"—something that in their view is concrete and developed in a rational process which can be interrupted at particular intervals for review and comment. The good-governmment groups are concerned about equity, order, and openness in government and pursue these objectives by being informed, civic-minded, and involved in the "participatory process."

Good-government groups can rarely help a public manager in any fundamental way—in an eleventh-hour labor negotiation with prison guards, having the League of Women Voters on your side is not likely to carry much clout—but they can hurt by virtue of the ability to discreetly criticize and spread the word about a manager's obstinacy, recalcitrance, or generally antagonistic attitude. Such damage to a manager's reputation may not hurt in the short run, but it will eventually reduce the manager's effectiveness.

The most important fact about good-government groups is that their real power is limited—at least in terms of political organization and "turning out the troops." But their financial power and political influence can still be significant. They pride themselves on their nonpartisanship, integrity, and good sense. Good-government groups usually have paid staffs, but their influence and reputation depend far more on their boards of directors and voluntary leaders. More often than not the people who join these groups are successful and, out of a sense of civic duty or real concern, believe that participation in public affairs is important.

Individual members of good-government groups may have very real concerns about the issues of the day, but these issues are seldom central to their personal health or well-being (contrast a welfare mother who joins a tenant rights organization with a suburban lawyer promoting open candidate forums for the county board races). Individual members of these groups may also have substantial political influence by virtue of professional position or family status.

Relatively speaking, the good-government groups are unfocused in their interests. They pursue no single issue, represent no specific constituency, and have no absolute criteria for supporting or opposing public officials or managers.

For the public manager, good-government groups can be frustrating because they may not comprehend that policy is made by a hundred different people in a hundred different ways every day or because their concerns sometimes seem less immediate, dramatic, or relevant than those of other pressure groups. But they can also help enormously by building support in areas politicians cannot reach, prompting the occasional positive editorial, and promoting the credibility and competence of the manager who has earned their respect. By and large, good-government groups are the most tame pressure groups with whom the manager must deal, and their causes, interests, and concerns rarely hurt the business of government. Coping with these interests is as much a matter of good judgment and open process as anything else.

Coping with good-government groups is considerably easier (albeit less interesting) than dealing with community organizations. Your objective with good-government groups is to make them love you while expending the minimum amount of your and your agency's time. This is not always easy, but the following guidelines can help.

Don't spend time cultivating members unless they wear two hats.

Many representatives of good-government groups have political and professional relevance for your agency quite apart from their role with their organization. For example, if the chair of the local Citizens Coalition for Participatory Government also happens to be the director of the largest private human services agency in the city, you might be well advised to be a little more available than you would be if he or she had no other relationship to your job. This is not to suggest that managers should be strictly self-serving in their dealings with good-government groups. Instead it means that time spent in conversation with good-government types should be as productive as possible and— whenever possible—should promote agency interests above and beyond the good-government issue.

Provide information regularly and often.

Good-government groups have a primary concern with staying informed—about what government is doing, when it is doing it, and why it is choosing to act as it does. Regular information on agency activities can be provided in person—which is time-consuming and occasionally less than constructive—or it can be provided through regular newsletters, updates, and media spots. The latter is far preferable and should serve to minimize the demands for private meetings from the good-government groups.

Be courteous and friendly.
Don't peddle the members to underlings.

If regular communications channels are established but good-government representatives still insist on personal audiences, see them; be polite and be interested.

Foisting good-government groups off on subordinates will only affront them, make your staff miserable, and increase the chance for misunderstanding, negative opinions, and demands for further meetings. Better to be available and civil than to compound the problem by being evasive, absent, and uninterested.

Inform, yes; consult, no.

Never consult good-government groups unless they specifically request it. Keep them informed about agency activities but do not solicit their involvement unnecessarily. If they have a matter to discuss with you, they will let you know. Because their interests are generally unfocused, it is better to let them define their issues than to invite their involvement and spend time that might not have been required.

If they become oppressive,
give them a specific task;
they'll usually disappear quietly.

If good-government groups are becoming pests and you simply cannot shake them, outline a specific issue and seek their participation in the solution. The more mundane and tedious the task, the quicker the effect. Members of good-government groups rarely have time to become deeply involved in a single issue or task. By holding them accountable for a concrete part of a solution you may stretch their commitment to the problem beyond the limit and they will usually fade away. If they stick to it and actually do what you have assigned, more power to them—it is free help and shows that they have more than a casual interest in your problems and are worth cultivating.

Above all, remember that good-government groups are not usually destructive. If they are sincerely interested in your agency and its problems, being nice and communicative cannot hurt. If only mildly interested, they will leave you alone providing you keep them informed and pester you only if you go out of your way to be evasive, arrogant, or nasty. Stay calm, be civil, and flood them with information—then get back to work.

SINGLE-ISSUE GROUPS: ONE STRIKE AND YOU'RE OUT

The third type of pressure group—and in many ways the toughest—is the single-issue or "special interest" group. These organizations form in response to a specific issue or problem and, unlike good-government groups or community groups with broad interests, they are highly focused and tenacious. Regardless of your track record or skill, if you aren't with the special interest group on their issue, they're against you. The opposite, however, is also true: if you happen to be on their side they can be powerful and productive allies.

Single-issue groups usually mean business. People do not normally join such groups for long-run prestige and power, although the publicity they generate often propels their leaders into prominent positions. Members of single-issue groups are often participating in their first form of organized political action, and they take the job seriously and passionately.

Single-issue groups know how to work hard, and they do not shy away from doing it. Their reward is not prestige but success—bending the government's actions to their view, their solution, or their philosophy. They are in it for the substance, and they are willing to do what is necessary to make sure their position prevails.

From the public manager's point of view, single-issue groups can be very rough. They will not tolerate foot-dragging, vacillation, or evasion. Because they are motivated by a belief in the righteousness of their cause (not necessarily its expediency), they have a tendency to allow the end to justify the means.

Single-issue groups are sophisticated strategists well attuned to the power of the media, large numbers of members, and big-name support. No tea and crumpets lobbyists here—this is the real stuff. Single-issue groups know the power of coalitions and are not reluctant to barter their organizational base in order to gain increased influence and exposure. They know the power of the grass roots, and they realize that members—the more the better—do not materialize out of thin air, but need recruiting, proselytizing, and good local organization.

Single-issue groups run the entire philosophical gamut. Once the darling of the liberals (abortion reform, civil rights, the women's movement), this form of pressure group activism is increasingly visible on the right. If the recent decade is any indication, the importance of the special interest and single-issue groups in the public manager's world will only increase, and the skill to cope productively with them will be a precious commodity.

Single-issue pressure groups are either with you or against you; there is rarely an in-between. Unfortunately many government officials make little distinction between those who are allies and those who are adversaries—they would rather not deal with single-issue groups at all. If the pressure groups share the public manager's philosophy and objectives, they can and should be considered assets. They should be brought into the solution, given some responsibility, and developed as part of a public / private partnership of promote the agency's mission. Single-issue groups are usually willing to be part of the solution, especially if government on its own does not have the capacity to perform, publicize, or organize a service in the way the group desires. This inclination to follow through and pitch in is what makes single-issue groups such potentially valuable assets to the public manager.

An example of how well this kind of partnership can work occurred with regard to the abortion issue in New York State. In the spring of 1970, the New York State Legislature made it legal for women to have an abortion up to twenty-four weeks into the pregnancy.

In the spring of 1970 the proponents of legal abortion were not at all convinced that the City was an ally in assuring broad access to safe abortions at the lowest possible cost. Some feared that the public hospitals, through inertia or design, would not meet the demand among city residents, particularly the poor, and that other health facilities would be swamped by nonresident demand. Others were convinced that Health Code provisions governing abortion would be overly restrictive, thus stifling the growth of free-standing clinics and requiring high-cost, in-hospital abortions.

I knew we were not going to let this happen, but it was vital that others know, too. I began in late spring of 1970 a series of meetings with the Abortion Coalition, a group comprising key representatives from organizations including Planned Parenthood, the National Association for Repeal of Abortion Laws, the Clergy Consultation Service on Abortion, Community Service Society, Women's City Club, and others. We discussed our problems openly and welcomed monitoring by these concerned groups. We took complaints about such problems as long waiting times at municipal hospitals not as unwelcome intrusions but as guides to action in perfecting our referral and service systems—and then reported on the status of those actions. We briefed these groups extensively on our strategy for promoting a network of high-quality, free-standing clinics by providing technical assistance in meeting Health Code requirements for clinics that seemed conscientious in their efforts. We were as tough as possible with others, short of precipitating closings that would threaten the "supply" side of the supply-demand equation.

We got feedback from the groups on how this strategy was working. We joined with them and others in fighting state attempts to cut back on Medicaid coverage. We testified at legislative hearings in opposition to any retreat from the new law. We provided data to help spread the word nationally on the success of the New York experience. One of my deputies chaired a committee to oversee

*operations of the Family Planning Information Ser-
vice, established as the City's largest free abortion
referral unit by Planned Parenthood of New York
City in close cooperation with HSA.*

*This openness and cooperation paid off in a
number of ways. First, we were able to use someone else's resources to help make our program go.
The Abortion Coalition frequently used its own
people to test the system for which we were responsible. They would send women into hospitals to sign
up for an abortion to see how long the waiting
period was, and they followed up on women who
had had abortions to see what kind of treatment
they received. If they had not helped with this
chore, I would have had to assign many of my
people to check on the system. Since the system
was performing at the rate of 200,000 abortions per
year, it would not have been easy or cheap to install
a good monitoring system. Nor would it have been
as trustworthy, because while my employees might
have been loath to uncover the frailties of their colleagues, the Abortion Coalition was not. Therefore I
got an ad hoc monitoring system which made it
possible to reduce our monitoring efforts and was
more trustworthy as well.*

*It also meant that when the Abortion Coalition
uncovered bad performance we had to correct the
deficiencies. We met periodically to hear the complaints, and I pushed very hard to make sure that
the deficiencies were corrected as fast as they
were uncovered.*

*We were able eventually to gain the respect of
the Abortion Coalition because our basic views
about abortion coincided with theirs, and because
we delivered. We dispelled the suspicion and
distrust of those who had fought long and hard for*

liberalized abortion and feared they would lose their legislative gains through administrative iner- tia or ineptness. When we said we were going to fix a deficiency in the system, we broke our backs to do it, and they knew it.

If single-issue groups are against you, you will need all of your political and professional resources to meet the challenge. Attempts at persuasion and compromise are futile, as these groups have highly focused objec- tives. As manager your only recourse is to rally the troops, display whatever muscle you can, and be decisive and consistent in your position.

If you and your chief are secure enough politically, the best course may be to ignore the groups that oppose you—weather the media campaign that is sure to be waged against you and stick to your guns. Few public of- ficials can hold out for long in the face of a determined campaign by highly organized and resourceful interest groups. If you can you should try to beat them at their own game—outorganize and outpublicize them. If this fails, hunker down and do the best you can while you still have the job. Public opinion is fickle, and if you hold out while at the same time holding up the standards of your agency, you may well win out in the long run.

6 / The Manager and the Media

People know what they know about their government primarily from what they read in the newspapers, what they hear on the radio, and what they see on television. For most people—citizens, voters, and officials alike—there is simply too much going on at too many levels of government to have firsthand knowledge of the full range of public activities. It is left to the media, those intrepid defenders of the public's right to know, to bridge the gap between personal experience with government and general ignorance of it. That many people's opinions about government are formed from morning headlines and occasional exchanges with government clerks—most often at the traffic ticket bureau or the tax assessor's—gives many a manager pause and suggests that the odds of developing a good reputation for you and your agency are only fair to slim.

The media's reach is awesome. Millions of Americans have televisions and radios, and almost everyone reads some newspapers and newsmagazines. This includes not only voters and clients of government services but judges, chief executives, legislators, community organizers, and other officials as well. The whole network of a public manager's colleagues, bosses, supporters, and opponents is influenced by the news, and more than any other actors in the manager's world the media can make or break an official overnight.

MEDIA CHARACTERISTICS

By tradition and by law the media are autonomous—not of government but not apart from it either. The press is often perceived as the fourth branch of government, with enormous influence over public policy, selection of public officials, and election of public leaders. And yet its quality controls are almost exclusively internal, and it is an enterprise beyond regulation and highly sensitive about outside criticism. While this is as it should be—the free press is an essential element of democracy—it is sometimes damn frustrating for public managers and elected officials. The press can hold government accountable through public exposure, but it can also vilify or at least cast suspicion on the character, motives, and decisions of almost any public official. Those in public life are ill positioned to counter poor-quality reporting, biased analysis, or unsubstantiated personal attack. Nevertheless, for public managers the press is as much a necessary ally as it is an irritating menace, and the ability to manage media relations successfully is among a public manager's most precious skills.

The media have two basic functions: to report the news and to inform the public. Depending on the level of government, the function of their agency, their relative power and prestige, and their personal style, public managers will deal with the media to varying degrees on both scores.

While many a journalist can wax eloquent on the media's responsibility to provide "all the news that's fit to print," public managers and their subordinates had better bear in mind a basic fact: the media are in business to make money—to sell newspapers, to entertain, to get good ratings, and to attract advertisers. And what sells is not the story that you, terrific public manager, were able to hold together fourteen thousand employees and millions of dollars of public funds for one more day without a crisis (while also making someone healthier). What sells is that a bureaucrat embezzled a thousand dollars from a government contract, that you and the budget chief hate each other's guts, and that ten more heroin addicts have overdosed, even though your agency is now treating ten thousand more addicts than you treated a year ago. The mentality that bad news is more profitable than good news goes for the industry as a whole, and it is certainly true for ambitious, young beat reporters and cynical, wizened city hall scribes who may go to excess to foster (if not manufacture) a good fight or scandal to liven up the morning news.

The news business is highly competitive. Reporters compete for by-lines, for air time, for big scoops, and for major stories. From the public manager's perspective, media relations are no less competitive. Elected and appointed officials are in competition for the "good news" space—always pretty limited—and for "subject" space as well. Local health news is just not as sexy as local crime news; city council elections are not as dramatic as presidential elections; and interstate disputes not as appealing as international disputes. It is not by chance that some public officials regularly get positive coverage and exposure for their agencies and programs. It is, instead, a sign of highly organized and systematic press operations.

Of course the media do not scrutinize all public

officials equally. Their attention will fall on those who by virtue of their power, position, or personality are likely to create controversy and crisis, or those who have become objects of controversy through scandal or investigation.

Public managers should also remember that the media are by nature skeptical about what government says about itself. Press releases, government reports, or evaluation studies can as easily look like propaganda as like public information. In light of this skepticism, getting stories published about agency accomplishments—instead of just failures—is extremely challenging. Many reporters are too busy with a crisis or major "bad news" piece to track down and check a positive release from an agency. Others are just too lazy to bother: with bad news lots of folks come to them; good news takes a little more effort. But good things do happen in government—addicts get treated, pregnant mothers get prenatal care, schoolchildren get fed, housing projects get built, highways and train tracks and buses get repaired—and it can certainly be argued that the public has as much right, if not as much desire, to be as informed about these events as about others.

Another important factor for managers to remember as they ponder their media operations is the tendency for time lag in covering nonsensational government news. Hundreds and hundreds of "newsworthy" items happen every day. The press has neither the space nor the reporters to cover them all. Just as bad news is more common than good, really bad news edges out your run-of-the-mill variety. If you as a manager take over an excellent agency and let it deteriorate slowly, with no major crisis, it may take six months or a year for anyone to notice. Similarly, if you take over a disaster and work miracles, it may also take that long. The inability of the press to cover all actions of government (good or bad) means that managers have considerable flexibility in their press relations. Averting agency crises will usually avert media attention. It may at least buy time to help ensure that overall agency performance is high once the press gets to your door.

The old adage that one should "never hit a man when he's down" is rarely the order of the day in the public sector. It is more common for officials to feel that the rule is "never hit a man unless he's down"; or, worse still, "always hit a man when he's down." It is an inescapable fact of public life that bad news follows an official like a stray puppy. The more there's been, the more you'll get. As a colleague once remarked, "Once they've seen you naked in public, it's hard for people to remember you with your clothes on." This means that there are personal as well as political and professional reasons for wanting positive coverage of your agency and program. Many an official's public career has been halted, sometimes very unfairly, by the media's characterization of the official's views or decisions. While clean hands are obviously the best defense, they are many times not enough; the reach of the media is just too great, and the damage that can be done by an erroneous accusation may be almost as serious as that by a deserved accusation. Establishing a rapport with the press which makes them more likely to take care in criticizing you and less likely to shoot from the hip at the first hint of trouble takes time and conscious effort. It does not come just from wearing a white hat.

The media provide the essential battleground for government affairs. Officials debate, constituents complain, special interests advocate, and managers defend in the columns of dailies and pages of weeklies; on the morning, afternoon, and evening news; and over radio's airwaves. Debates between branches of government, among officials within each branch, and between the government and the public are daily occurrences which are dictated in large part by the choices made by editors and reporters about what is interesting and what is relevant for their subscribers to know. For all these reasons—the nature of the media; the importance of the media to a manager's relationship with colleagues, bosses, and constituents; and the difficulty in directing the attention of the media to governmental success rather than failure—the manager's media relations, the last part of the manager's environment to be explored, are perhaps the most sensitive and unpredictable of all the professional relationships.

WHERE AND WHEN?
MANAGERS AND THE PRESS

They are seldom there when you want them and ever-present when you do not. They are always accurate and precise when it is unimportant, and superficial and misleading when it is not. There is always a world crisis dominating the news on days when you have good stories to report, and little happening when you are caught with your pants down. If ever there is a classic case of love-hate relationships in the public sector, it is between reporters and public managers. A manager is never so grateful as when the editorial page says "that commissioner is the best thing that's happened to state government in twenty-five years" and never so bitter as when the evening news reports you personally accountable for a crisis over which you had little control and no warning, let alone a chance to reply.

The public manager and the press can interact on all matters. No decision, no statement, no action, and no plan is beyond the purview of the media. A sensitivity to the media implications of any management decision—

internal or external—is essential for the skillful public manager. How might it look? How might it sound? Who is going to be happy? Who is going to be mad? Where are we vulnerable? Where are we strong?

The manager and the media will deal with each other on the manager's external relationships: with community groups, special interests, other branches of government, and even the chief. The press will be interested in those relationships—again in proportion to your power, performance, and personality—and will study and sometimes exploit them. A good round of name calling and dirt slinging between colleagues is always good fare; and the natural tensions, animosities, and competition among government officials will almost always find their way into the papers.

But just as the press can influence and sometimes determine the state of a manager's external relationships, it can also strongly influence internal agency administration and morale. Bad news can create internal dissension and low morale—especially if it is untrue or only partially true. Glowing coverage of the agency head, on the other hand, can also create tension and jealousy—especially when the manager appears to be gaining personal praise and attention for subordinates' contributions. Good news that credits the responsible staff can increase productivity and provide incentive for quality employees. If you like your name in the press, remember how much you would have liked it earlier in your career.

Media relations also help greatly in obtaining resources. An agency's public reputation—and that of the manager—does not go unnoticed by the agencies making funding decisions or juggling competing requests. No one responsible for handing out public funds wants to throw good money after bad. The most accessible measure of what is good and bad, and which officials are capable and which incompetent, is often what is written in the paper. Maintaining credibility with the chief executive, building power in the community, and establishing credibility with the legislature all depend largely on your public image as well as your professional performance.

The press is most likely to be watching you if your agency is involved in a crisis, if oversight or investigative hearings are under way or rumored, if labor negotations are going on, if special interests have assaulted you, or if a political campaign is in swing. At other times the manager can more easily control the media's access to agency affairs. The trick is to guide the media to your agency's best side and keep them away from the hot spots.

While much of the relationship between a manager and the media is unpleasant, there are also positive reasons for careful attention to press relations. The media can often be critical in program implementation. The most elegantly conceived and best-administered program is useless if no one knows about it. Fifty new prenatal clinics will not help expectant mothers if the mothers cannot find them; homeowners' tax credits will not make overburdened taxpayers happy if they do not know how to get them; special education programs will not help children if parents do not know they exist. Mass marketing is vital for many government programs, and the public manager depends greatly on the media for this. For managers whose agencies provide public services it is critical that a cooperative relationship be established with the print and electronic media.

Knowing that the press will likely be around every corner and that many of your programs may be more dependent than you had thought on the cooperation of the mass media is only a very preliminary step toward getting your media relations in order. You had better convince yourself that a good press operation is very important because you will have to devote considerable time and attention to developing one. Once you realize this, you can master the basics and develop a few tricks, which will increase the chance that the news you hear about your operation will be good news.

IMPRESSING THE PRESS: ORGANIZING YOUR MEDIA EFFORT

The public manager's strategy with the press is a simple one: get the good news out. Colleagues and co-workers have often asked why. It takes so much effort, they say—and it does—to get even a small story in the *New York Times*, the *Washington Post*, or the *Minneapolis Tribune* or any other newspaper or television news show. For instance, a story about the progress of a new alcoholism program is the result of a lot of work on the part of both program staff and the press department. The staff's progress report would be prepared anyway, to keep superiors and oversight bodies aware of project status; but the press department must turn that usually dull prose, facts, and figures into something lively, something that will catch the public's eye.

So the question why is a fair one. And its answer is pretty straightforward. First there is the general public. They watch and read and listen and care what happens around them. And they respond to news stories with action. They can vote your boss in or out; they can back your improvements or call for your head. Enough good or bad press can make a substantial difference in the general public's perception of you as a manager and your agency's programs. After all, most of the public judges your work from the press reports.

The special constituencies—community organizations and special interests—also have an interest in a particular part of your agency and program and can demand or provoke media coverage about their area of concern. Good press builds credibility with these people so that they are more likely to support or at least refrain from attacking your programs. If they can at least remember your name—if not your work—in a positive way, they are likely to go along with your next project. If they cringe at the mention of your name, they are likely to reject anything you propose, regardless of merits.

Good press evokes feelings of well-being at city hall, the governor's mansion, the White House, and even the offices of the local, state, and congressional representatives with whom you must deal. If the mayor or the governor follows your press, then it is, by definition, important.

Good press means you are likely to gain more money, staff, and facilities and to win policy disputes. Good press makes it easier to attract good people to your organization. Good people are always tough to come by, particularly in local government. Good press makes you and your agency seem exciting, and to the extent that it allows you to recruit better staff it will be a self-fulfilling prophecy. Good press also helps keep the vultures off your back. Critics, political opportunists, and rival politicians are less likely to use you for cannon fodder if you have a solid public reputation. And good press is good for your ego. People's reasons for making a career in public service are highly varied, but most public managers harbor at least a little (if not a lot) of ego, and there is no reason not to savor a little reward in the form of a positive story or a complimentary editorial.

So the rule is, if you don't get good press you are more likely to get bad press. If good press is money in the bank, the opposite is also true: when you look like a fool or a bad manager, when you are caught in a leaky operation or a lie, when you just plain get a bad story, that invisible Dun and Bradstreet goes down. You have to start drawing down credit, and that gets used up very fast in the public sector.

Subordinates often do not understand the reasons for wanting good press. They may consider the time and effort involved as wasted, may learn quickly to mistrust reporters and their editors, and may be in a poor position to see the indirect benefits accruing to the agency and administration as a whole from a successful press operation. Public managers must spend time creating among subordinates a respect for the importance of a solid press operation and the necessity to have some credibility when the inevitable bad news hits.

So how do you develop a workable press strategy?

Sooner or later you will get what you deserve from the media; your performance is the key.

No matter how sophisticated your press office, how large your publications budget, and how slick your public image, in the end it is your agency's performance that counts. In the public sector virtue is not its own reward. A good effort may be appreciated in the short run, but if you don't deliver it will soon be forgotten. Managers who run their programs poorly may be able to bluff colleagues, legislators, and even their chief executives for a time; but once the media has taken aim, you are unlikely to make it with only the facade of competence. Of course the media can be superficial and often fall for a good line, but no one can consistently ignore job performance and maintain a good and professional public reputation. If you run a lousy operation you deserve bad press, and you will get it. Being competent is not in and of itself a sure road to good press, but being bad is a certain path to negative stories.

Know yourself, and make sure your press people know you too.

Public managers are seldom miracle workers or superhumans. We are all good at some things, passable at others, and miserable at still others. As a manager you must spend time honestly assessing your strengths and weaknesses.

Not every manager's style is the same and not every manager can pull off interviews and press conferences. The important thing is to approach media relations in a way that makes you feel comfortable. Your efforts will succeed only if your press staff knows you well and you are candid with them about what you can and cannot do. Do not let your media consultant talk you into a television spot that you feel certain you cannot handle. Project only an honest image of yourself. You got where you are because you have important strengths and skills. It is these qualities—not someone else's idea of what qualities would be nice—that have to be the foundation of your press strategy.

I tried to honestly consider my strengths and style and make sure that my press director knew me. (In fact, I married her. This is not recommended in all cases.) My tone was not the same as everyone else's. For example, Naomi Feigelson, my press chief, worked for New York City's consumer affairs commissioner, Bess Myerson, before she worked for me, and she approached it differently. To begin with, Bess was a former Miss America. That embarrassed Bess, and she often tried to live it down because she was serious and did serious things in public office. But she was nevertheless a very attractive lady—theatrical, glamorous, and a professional at TV. She had a lighter touch, and in her

press she could make her point and get away with a
kind of humor that would fall from me like lead.

Organize the press operation carefully.
Do not divorce it from agency programs,
policy, and administration.

No matter how small your agency is, press operations
are not an ad hoc affair. In some governments it is possible to centralize press operations, to provide press
services from an office of communication or a similar
shared resource that serves a number of agencies and
managers at once. In others, however, the manager is
forced—by the size of the agency, the nature of the
agency's operation, or the lack of adequate press operations at the top—to organize his or her own press unit.

The most common mistake made by managers and
public officials is to isolate the press operation from the
rest of the agency. To set the press officer to the side ac-
complishes little. To be able to market the agency's good
news and field the hailstorm when there is bad, the
press chief and staff must understand you and understand what you are up against in your agency.

The press officer not only has to know the operation
but has to be aggressive at seeking out the "good news"
items and angles. If your press staff wait for line
managers to bring them stories, they are unlikely to get
anything useful.

A wide-ranging, active, and involved press operation
can have other benefits for you as a manager as well.
The press people bring a different perspective to agency
programs than do your professionals or line workers.
The press staff can see things, and often hear things,
that might not otherwise surface in the pressures of
day-to-day management. Because they are looking for
good stories and trying to prepare for bad news, their in-

vestigations can give you a kind of monitoring of staff performance which does not come from regular channels. In other words, your press staff and public information people can serve as watchdogs. You can never have too many of these in your own house. Of course this can be dangerous and tricky as well. Subordinates may resent the press staff's opinions about how they and their programs are doing. They may feel threatened by probing and inquisitive press aides and consider themselves under surveillance rather than objects of potential publicity. As a manager it is important to cultivate the staff's acceptance of your press people and to make clear, at every opportunity, that the press operation is an integral, professional part of your agency's team. Making sure that as many compliments as criticisms get translated down the line as a result of press staff inquiries should help maintain the balance between internal resentment and support for your press strategy.

When the abortion laws in New York City were new, there were frequent charges that city hospitals were not responding properly, that women were not referred promptly, that there were inexcusable waiting periods. My own staff handling the program insisted that things were not "that bad." So I had the public information staff make some fifty calls to our referral service, posing as women wanting appointments, and then go to the hospitals and check them out. It turned out that in many cases the complaints were valid.

I called in the people running the abortion program and showed them our own reports. It was hard for them to deny that kind of evidence. They didn't like it, of course, but they had to respond. It's a lot better to have your press director call attention to your foul-ups than the New York Times.

We did the same thing with birth certificates. We had installed a new information retrieval system which speeded up the time it took to get a birth certificate from five to eight weeks to a matter of days. We had announced it with great hoopla and publicized it all over, and still people were calling in complaining of long delays. The people who ran the program had had a lot of headaches and pointed out that there was still some room for error. But just to keep the heat on them to clean up the system as quickly as possible, I had those members of the public information staff born in New York City write or come in for certificates to test how long it took.

I felt it was very important to make sure those things were going right. On the merits it was right. Also, it will catch up with you if they don't go right. And inevitably someone like the managing editor of the Daily News *will write in for a birth certificate and it will take three weeks. If you've said it would take three days, you've had it. If I could help it I didn't like to wait for the public to discover our mistakes even if it meant a little staff resentment.*

Keep churning out material even if the response is slow.

For a good press strategy it is necessary to churn out as much well-written, well-designed material as humanly possible (and as your budget allows). The media (along with many of the other actors in your professional world) often complain that no one keeps them informed. Public managers have to find ways to counter that complaint while at the same time not boring them to death. And that's not easy.

Good writing ability (a sadly overlooked talent), an ability to get along with people (especially those special creatures who become reporters), a high energy level, and a creative mind are minimum requirements for a good press officer. Even if all of your releases, publications, and announcements are not used, they establish a public record of the accomplishments of the agency and will ultimately serve you well. A press chief who continually designs new and better ways to channel this material to the outside world will be worth his or her weight in gold. Even if resources are strapped and program pressures and administrative demands enormous, the skillful manager will find a way to keep the information flowing. As a means of preparing for the next public affairs crisis, there is simply no substitute.

Don't be afraid of numbers— they won't bite, and the public is not so unsophisticated as you think.

Many public managers avoid facts and figures in their press releases like the plague. While it is true that ten pages of tables can be boring and incomprehensible, it is also true that details on how 20,000 addicts were treated are much more impressive than general news that addicts were treated. You should not be afraid to quantify agency accomplishments, to give detailed breakdowns on numbers of clients served, revenues raised, resources saved, or offenders caught.

There are only two measures of program success— quality and quantity—and the only way to measure quantity is with numbers. If you have tested more people for lead poisoning this year than last, or if you have rid more premises of garbage or increased the number of prison doctors by fifty percent, then say so. You are a lot more likely to get press coverage and a lot more likely to make people remember your work.

Remember that the press is skeptical about anything

you say, and broad generalizations about agency progress or successful programs are easily overlooked. Be explicit, show the data, and be ready to back them up with real-life stories about who those addicts were or what the project really involved.

Don't be cute or contrived. It will hurt more than help.

Reporters are busy people and so are public managers. There is nothing more irritating to either side than media gambits which are hyped up or staged only for ego gratification. Do not hold a press conference if a news release will suffice. Do not confuse your press conference with your wish to look important, or confuse your presentation with that of a mayor or governor in terms of importance to the press. Elected officials command media attention because there are always plenty of political questions to be asked. The press only wants to ask you as a public administrator why you brought them out on a rainy day. You better have a good answer, because reporters and photographers have very long memories.

Do not hustle all across the state when a TV spot could as easily and just as effectively be taped in your own office. Like any other group with whom the manager deals, the press should never be antagonized unnecessarily. Making them work harder or expend more resources than necessary to get a story is sure to put you on the enemies list.

Of course this does not mean that you should never go on location or up to the podium to argue your own case. Sometimes the power behind a story rests in its immediacy and in providing reporters with a real-life sense of what you are doing, whom you are doing it for, and why it is necessary. The rule is not to stay indoors and drone on; rather, it is to be selective about dramatic effects, to avoid histrionics, and to make sure you accommodate the media's time constraints and resource limits as much as possible.

> *A trip to the Tombs (New York City's detention center) was enough to make you crazy if you weren't already. It reminded me of everything I'd read of the early French prisons and insane asylums, the Bedlams. It was bedlam—the noise, the screaming, the lack of privacy, the hands reaching out through the bars. It was earsplitting and mind-rending just to walk through there. The prospect of actually being confined there was sickening. The idea of actually helping people under these conditions was staggering. To get that across to the press was important, and it wasn't something that could be done from behind my desk. So I took them out there and let them see conditions first hand. Some were plenty scared, but the point was made and the stories reflected it.*

Look at a problem—and schedule— from the reporter's perspective. Be accommodating.

Reporters have bosses and deadlines and colleagues and competitors like anyone else. While public managers will seldom admit that reporters are human, they are. To the extent that you and your staff convey a sense of cooperation and accommodation in your dealings with the media, they are likely to reciprocate, at least occasionally.

This means that you should not, as a general rule, avoid returning a reporter's call until just after the afternoon deadline or a TV journalist's inquiry until just after airtime. It means that you should not keep reporters waiting, treat them discourteously, or otherwise make their lives miserable just because of your general wariness of their motives and character.

You should also be sure that releases are well written and comprehensive. If possible they should have something that will catch the eye of the assignment editor, who sees scores of releases every day. Remember that releases are inputs—the outputs are stories. Emphasize to your press staff that if there's a chance for something to go wrong in the process of turning a release into a story, it will; the only way to prevent problems is through rigorous follow-up and anticipation.

Call the reporter a day or two ahead of time if possible. Tell the reporter that the release is coming, why it is important, and when to expect it. Be sure the release gets into the reporter's hand promptly. Once the reporter reads it, see if any more information is needed. You cannot make a reporter write a story or an editor print it. But you sure can lead a horse to water.

Of course, timing is important. Monday is a good day to shoot for because news coverage is often lighter over the weekend and Monday circulation tends to be high. Saturdays are bad because circulation is low. Learn the cycles of your reporters as well as those of your own staff. You will be amazed how this information can improve the productivity of your press operation.

Of course, some reporters ask for bad treatment. The golden rule tends to be a principle in practice as well as thought when it comes to media relations: do unto reporters as they do unto you. Remember that they are notoriously thin-skinned, even while demanding that public officials suffer through all sorts of innuendo and rhetoric in silence. If reporters abuse their jobs, go out of their way to make excessive demands on your staff, or behave unpleasantly, they should be hauled on the carpet.

Anticipate the bad news, and beat the media to the punch when possible.

If you know that a crisis is about to hit—a bad audit, a personnel scandal, a program failure, or a political controversy—do not let the media get the jump on you and print their version first. Quickly put out your own release, state your version of the case, and stand by it. If the agency is at fault, accept the blame. Nothing takes the wind out of the sails of aggressive investigative reporters like getting scooped by the responsible agency. Few reporters know how to cope with managers who accept responsibility, provide quick and thorough action to meet problems, and engage in candor and responsiveness rather than evasion and subterfuge. You would be surprised how this can unnerve the press—and how much easier it can make your life.

> When I first came to HSA we did a staff study of prison health care which identified several significant problems: overcrowded, inadequate facilities, both for general care and narcotics abuse; inadequate staff; and divided responsibility. Not only was the overcrowding of detained people bad for health care, it was an inexcusable violation of civil liberties to keep someone in jail waiting longer for a determination of fitness than they might be kept if tried and found guilty.
>
> By early spring of 1971, we had outpatient clinics giving competency exams open or ready to open in all boroughs. In the Bronx and Manhattan, we had reduced to zero the number of people detained while waiting for exams to stand trial. We had reduced the capacity at Bellevue to normal, and after constant fights with the Correction Department, with General Services and the Bureau of the

Budget, we were close to opening a new prison psychiatric facility at Rikers Island.

We should have put that story out as soon as we had it, but my prison health staff wanted to wait until "we really had something done." I went along with them, and it turned out to be a big mistake on my part. Because later in the spring, a City Council committee decided to hold public hearings. Now the usual purpose of public hearings is to get good press for those holding them and to expose everyone else—in this case, HSA. Well, they did just that, using the same staff study we had prepared in October 1970 to beat us over the head with. I suspect that if I had had the brains to release that report when it was originally done, or had put out a couple of good stories between October 1970 and the spring of 1971, there might never have been a hearing at all.

That particular incident, though—as well as a more important hearing by the Board of Correction later on (where we were also killed)—did emphasize publicly a real problem, the fragmentation of services. The mayor resolved this in September 1971 by giving us responsibility for all prison health care. Until then, responsibility had been split between the Health Department, the Mental Health Department, the Health and Hospitals Corporation, and the Correction Department. In practice, that means a nurse who worked in the prisons was hired and fired by Correction but might report to a doctor who worked for Health. Doctors were paid by Health but fell, de facto, under Correction's control; and in Mental Health everyone except the chief psychiatrist worked for Correction. On top of the lousy working conditions (who wants to be in prison, even eight hours a day?) and the inferior pay, this made it incredibly hard to get decent staff and virtually impossible to keep them if they did come.

We eventually changed much of that. Once HSA got responsibility, we were able to put together the various fragments in a constructive way which made decent health care possible. We recruited first-rate people. We instituted new medical procedures upgrading the admission physical, sick call screening, and planned medication reviews. We upgraded and expanded the medical, nursing, and paraprofessional staff. We added VD tests for men and women to all admission physicals. We started a prison aftercare program and death review board to look carefully into all prison deaths so as to prevent them in the future.

I gave my press chief a few bad moments when I told my staff we were going to eliminate all prison deaths. She said, "Great, do it, but please don't tell anybody else." I was hardly grandiose enough to think we could wipe out death in prisons, not with 100,000 people going through a year. But I wanted to force my staff to knock themselves out reducing the number. Deaths did, in fact, drop from thirty-four in 1971 to about twenty in 1973.

We also introduced or greatly expanded such specialty services as dental care, eye care, chest surveys, and outpatient care and enlarged and improved the methadone detoxification program. But our greatest accomplishment was to negotiate contracts with hospitals to provide prison care voluntarily. By the time I left (and it took us two years to get it) we had signed a contract with Montefiore Hospital, one of the best hospitals in the country, to provide medical care for sixty percent of the prisoners in New York City.

The first people who noticed were the prisoners. Larry Blyden (one of the Attica rebels and leader of the Tombs riots in 1970) told Jack Newfield of the Village Voice on a TV program that the prison situation in general was still horrible, but the health care in the New York City prisons had improved a lot. Among other things, he said the nurses even smiled now at the prisoners. We even began to get letters from inmates. Then we knew we were on the way.

And we began putting out stories about what we had done. After those first experiences as the target in someone else's sights, we realized we had better get some money in the bank before that happened again.

In the end, even the national press recognized it. In its July 9, 1973 issue, Time magazine, after a survey on prison health care around the United States, cited New York City as having made "the greatest strides [in the country] . . ." in delivering health care in prisons.

Capitalize on advocacy functions— they make good news.

If your agency has advocacy responsibilities—enforcement of consumer standards, licensing and inspection of facilities, enforcement of regulations, advocacy for special client groups—capitalize on them in your press strategy. Advocacy issues make good copy; people like to read about how many of the bad guys were caught even if the good guys in the story were government officials. These types of stories also have great potential for human interest angles—for profiling the tenant saved from eviction after refusing to pay rent because of no heat or water, or the handicapped child who finally gets to go to a regular school because special education services have been required. While good news space is limited, this is the kind of story that often catches the media's eye. If you are lucky enough to run an agency that can boast these kinds of successes, publicize them regularly. It is always best to be on the side of the avenging angels.

At Health Services Administration, our number one headline grabber was what came to be called our Dirty Restaurant List. It's also a good example of how the press can make a public administrator do what he ought to do.

The Health Department, which was mandated to inspect all restaurants for health code violations, was in the process of revamping its inspection system in the summer of '71 when Scanlon's, a short-lived muckraking magazine, ran an article by New York Post reporter Joe Kahn rating several fancy New York eateries not with stars but with garbage cans. The story caused a sensation. Joe's rating was based on an inspection tour with one of our health inspectors, and in this case the visual expression—the garbage cans—was what made the story sink in.

John Sibley, who was then covering the health beat for the New York Times, thought we should be doing the same thing. He urged us to publish a list of health code violators, and he blasted us for our secrecy in the Times. We were concerned about the fairness of such publicity, perhaps ruining a business for all time after one listing. We also had to consider the confidentiality issue versus the public's right to know. But after deliberating we decided that the new inspection system itself ensured fairness. If a restaurant failed two inspec-

tions and could not show good cause at a department hearing, surely the public had the right to know. We informed all the restaurants, and we also told them we'd publish their names when they cleared up the violations if they wanted us to.

We notified the media that a restaurant list would soon be routinely forthcoming. The Times ran it the next day and every list from then on, as did all the papers. Lucille Rich of CBS-TV made it a household word by reciting it twice a week on the 6 o'clock news against the background of appropriate mood music and a rat climbing out of a garbage can waving a wooden spoon. But it was the list's popularity—the public liked it—that made it part of the New York landscape.

We probably had more mail and more publicity on our restaurant list than on anything else besides abortions. We had letters from people who came to New York frequently, asking for all the lists. We had postcards from New Yorkers telling us about dirty restaurants they had been in and asking us to inspect, which we did.

Of course, we had a lot of angry restaurant owners claiming we had ruined their business. But we had no lawsuits and no public reprisals from them because they had several chances to clean their own house before we labeled it dirty. Our system was uniform and scrupulously fair. It was lovely, for once, to be pointing the finger at someone else.

Don't be caught off guard— preparation is the best offense.

Reporters like nothing better than catching a manager unawares. Once you have been blind-sided by a clever journalist or cornered unwillingly at your local grocery store on Saturday, you will be much more sympathetic to the need to control reporters' access to you.

You need to establish a mechanism to screen reporter contacts. Standard operating procedures for how, when, and under what circumstances you—and your staff—will be available for press contacts should be shared with reporters beforehand so that there are no misunderstandings. A willingness to be responsive in a timely manner when a controversy does hit is essential, but reporters will accept your need to be prepared and ready for these contacts.

If you are caught unawares, resist the urge to speak extemporaneously. It is better to offer no comment, risking the inevitable criticism which reporters will level, and agree to call back later, than to make a misleading or inaccurate statement off the cuff. That is what they want you to do because contradictions make news. So use your head and do not leave yourself vulnerable.

As a public manager it is inevitable that one day you will wake up to see on the front page an internal agency memorandum, or a nasty note from you to a legislator, or a draft evaluation report which condemns half your agency. A neurotic public manager would never get anything accomplished, because he or she would never write anything down for fear of misuse or misinterpretation. It is not quite that bad, but it is surprising how frequently managers—and subordinates—fail to anticipate the media implications of a particularly controversial issue paper or internal agency report.

Government could not function if ideas and disagreements were not debated and discussed. It only takes a little common sense for you, and by way of your example your staff, to learn to be conscious of what you write and what you circulate. The rule is always to assume that a report or memorandum or letter could be made public, and to be sure that—if it must be written—it is professional, accurate, and responsible.

Never say anything to a reporter that you aren't willing to see in print.

Easier said than done. Most reporters respect confidentiality and a manager's request to go off the record or on background. But you cannot count on this. "Off the record" means very different things to different reporters, and you should be sure that you both mean the same thing up front. Novice managers often make the mistake of not being explicit about the nature of a press interview. Remember that it is what you say at the start that sets the rules of the game, not what you say after you have babbled for twenty minutes.

Like any other profession, journalism has some unscrupulous practitioners and some who are downright deceitful in their dealings with public officials. Some reporters may be too eager to get a story, others may feel that a story is just too big and important to honor all promises, and others may just have so little respect for public officials that they feel no compunction about using material provided in confidence.

There is only one rule in discussions with the press: do not say it if you do not want to see it. This rule will protect you, protect your relationship with the reporter, and may very well protect your relationship with the boss, your colleagues, or any of a number of other people with whom you must work.

Don't try to seduce the press— it simply doesn't work.

There is a strong temptation on the part of agency press relations people, especially if they have been on the other side, to feel shamefaced about their present occupation, to yearn for their adversary role, and to say things to reporters that they should not so they will be well liked. There is a strong temptation to try gimmicks to get reporters on your side; to be buddies, to feed information when possible, to try to buy them off in the long run with short-term favors and gratuities.

Forget it—it never works in the long run. Your performance can build up money in the bank, and deserved good press does provide some insurance against the inevitable bombshell. But favors and seductions cannot. And it is important not only for you to realize it but for your press staff to understand as well. Press officers and aides as well as administrative and program subordinates simply must accept that it will not help their cause to try to win over news reporters with attention, juicy inside gossip, or other tactics. Reporters have very, very short memories when it comes to favors granted, and the practice will almost always backfire.

Pay as much attention to your public information campaigns as to your news operations.

Public information is public outreach. It is a way to enhance both the stature and the effectiveness of your agency. Public information—getting out the details of program services, eligibility requirements, new initiatives—is no less important than generating good news and is often crucial to program success. Your media staff should anticipate the information that people will need about a program before they have to call and ask. You have to sell programs. That means you not only have to let people know where they could go for a service, but often have to convince them that it is a good idea for them to have their blood pressure taken, to be treated for VD, to get rid of their heroin addiction, or to vaccinate their children. While most people have now been brainwashed into buying soap, waxes, deodorants, and all kinds of other often unnecessary cleaners, they are not yet convinced, for example, that it is necessary to be screened for VD or hypertension. So you have to be persuasive as well as informative.

And don't forget the radio. I had been very skeptical of radio spots at the beginning and did them more to humor my press chief than for anything else. I saw it as throwing your message to sea in a bottle. Nobody listens to radio, I told her; but her answer was that everybody does.

I soon began to hear that from all over—people who listen to the radio in the car, people who wake up at night and turn on the radio, people who stay home and always have something going in the background. People would tell me they woke up at 3:00 A.M. to hear "This is Gordon Chase, New York City Health Services Administrator, with a message about your VD."

Radio stations are required by the FCC to do public service announcements. They cost us little to produce, and it was much easier for me to read with expression than to mug on TV. It was great for our public information operation.

Of course when the public does make inquiries, the agency's response should be quick, courteous, and thorough. Public requests to an operating agency should be treated as seriously as constituent requests to elected officials. Your capacity to respond contributes greatly to your public image and credibility. Besides filling a real need, the quick response has an immediate payoff. Any citizen who gets a fast answer from the bureaucracy is thunderstruck. And then grateful. And then word gets around.

When the bad news hits, assess the damage and calculate the response.

It is going to happen to you sooner or later if you make a career in public life. If you are lucky you will have a little forewarning, will have the resources or capacity to respond, and will be able to come out of the crisis intact, if a little the worse for wear.

The most important thing is to think through your responses and not overreact. A brief story on page 50 may infuriate you, but you may do more damage by responding than by letting it go. Turning a one-day headache into a week-long battle has no payoff. If the story is major and poses a real threat to your job, program, or staff, then a response is certainly necessary; but it is essential that it be professional, carefully documented, and objective, and that you avoid stooping to the level of your accusers.

If the attack is a personal one, it is best to resist the urge—if at all possible—to respond yourself. It is much more effective to let your supporters and colleagues present your case for you. You avoid the appearance of self-interest and the inevitable indiscretions that may come from your own emotionalism and wounded pride. Your own response is naturally biased. All of the work you have put into building a relationship with your chief, with the community, with legislators, with overhead agencies, and with special interests is intended to pay off on these occasions. Allies are not necessary if you are unwilling to rely on them during a crisis. Let them do the talking; you, your agency, and your case will be the better for it.

Above all else tell the truth.

If anyone in your entire working world is likely to catch you in a lie, an evasion, or a "mistruth," it is the press. There is simply no reason to expose yourself to this situation. Whatever the problem you think you are solving by a lie, it will only be made worse in the end. Reporters want to catch you, the public likes to see this, and your enemies will enjoy it; so what is the point? Never, never, never lie.

So with the media it is simple: remember that everything you say and do is potentially of interest to the media. Be smart, be circumspect; do not pull surprises or double-cross your friends in print through intentional or unintentional remarks; and remember that the media provide your primary vehicle for communicating with your ultimate employer—the public. Use the media to advantage and as an asset to maintain good programs and good administration.

Epilogue:
Managers and
Perspective

I can remember, when I first became administrator of the New York City Health Services Administration (the first nonphysician to hold that position), that I would call in my commissioners and senior managers and ask them what they'd been doing—what their agencies or units or programs had been up to in the last few weeks or months or years.

Some of these senior officials would start by telling me how many meetings they had attended, how many memos they'd written, how many staff they'd hired, and similar benchmarks of bureaucratic activity. I'd look at them and say: "But whom did you make healthy today (or last week, or last year)? Did you make anybody in New York healthier—and how do you know?"

In short order people came to realize where I wanted my emphasis—not on the mechanics of running public agencies but on the outcome of the services we were there to deliver. It's not that I didn't understand the importance of dealing with the *chief, overhead agencies, and the rest of the characters in our daily fare; it's just that I wanted the right perspective—I wanted my managers to be conscious of the fact that we were there to make people healthier, and not to lose sight of that fact in the daily squabblings that we all had to endure.*

No one can predict with certainty what will make a good public manager. No single combination of education, experience, personality, and talent will make the same person a great commissioner of welfare for New York City and a smashing water and sewer director in Seattle. Each state, city, county, and township has a unique set of political, social, and economic challenges to which an aspiring public manager must adapt.

But, as the preceding chapters have suggested, there are predictable problems, dilemmas, conflicts, and confrontations that are sure to occur at some point, to some degree, in every public manager's life. There is one thing that is certain: a manager's view of his or her mission will be the key to success in the public world.

Charisma, rhetoric, and good public relations, while sometimes crucial to a particular problem or issue, are not sufficient to sustain a public manager. Performance—the ability to deliver against multiple odds, and to deliver quickly and consistently—is what matters.

If a manager's mission is to promote a given politician or a particular ideology but services are poorly managed and people (our clients) are poorly served, then what is the point? As manager, your mission must be, first and foremost, to make government work—to decide what values you have, how they relate to government's role, how that translates into government programs, and how you can make those programs work. With that perspective in hand, an aspiring or a veteran manager can make judgments about where to work, whom to work for, and how to tackle the environment.

Sitting behind the desk, meeting with interest after interest, fighting against another round of red tape with the budget bureau, and listening to one more lecture from a twenty-two-year-old on the governor's staff, all make maintaining perspective a challenge in itself. Public management is not a profession for the faint of heart, for those who want always to be loved and admired, or for those who think there is nothing to running the public's business but a little common sense and acumen. It is tough work, and its rewards are often ambiguous, but they are by no means nonexistent.

This book is intended to provide a few bromides for the mental, emotional, and occasionally physical indigestion that comes from coping with the manager's world. In the end the best advice is straightforward and simple:

Stay honest, be smart, and care—the public will be the better for it.

ABOUT THE AUTHORS

GORDON CHASE served in numerous capacities in the federal, state, and local government.

After graduating from Harvard College in 1954, Mr. Chase joined the Marine Corps and subsequently entered the United States Foreign Service. Following assignments in Pakistan and England, Chase returned to the United States to serve McGeorge Bundy on the staff of the National Security Council.

In 1967 he was appointed Staff Director for the new Equal Employment Opportunity Commission. He later moved to New York City, becoming Deputy Director of the Human Resources Administration and then, in 1970, Administrator of the City's Health Services Administration. He was appointed to both of these positions by Mayor John V. Lindsay.

From 1974 until 1979 Mr. Chase was a lecturer and director in the executive management programs of Harvard's John F. Kennedy School of Government and School of Public Health. During this period he also served on the faculty of the Florence Heller Graduate School for Advanced Studies in Social Welfare at Brandeis University.

In the fall of 1978 he served briefly as Massachusetts Secretary of Human Services, a position to which he was appointed by Governor Michael Dukakis.

At the time of his death in January of 1980, Gordon Chase held a tenured faculty position at the Florence Heller Graduate School for Advanced Studies in Social Welfare at Brandeis University.

ELIZABETH C. REVEAL has spent ten years in state and local government in Minnesota, the District of Columbia, and New York. A participant in the 1979 Program for Senior Executives in State and Local Government at Harvard, she returned to the Kennedy School in the fall of 1980 to complete the Chase manuscript and to participate in the school's Mid-Career Public Administration Program.

Ms. Reveal graduated from Cornell University in 1971 and holds master's degrees from the University of Michigan and Harvard University. She is presently working in the field of municipal finance and budgeting.

ABOUT THE CONTRIBUTORS

GRAHAM T. ALLISON, JR. is Don K. Price Professor of Politics and Dean of the John F. Kennedy School of Government, Harvard University. Dean Allison is widely regarded for his work on foreign policy decision making—in particular, his book *Essence of Decision*. His current research and teaching interests are concentrated in the areas of political analysis, American foreign policy, and ethics and public policy. Dean Allison is a member of the Trilateral Commission and a director of the Council on Foreign Relations, as well as a member of the Foreign Affairs Task Force of the Democratic Advisory Committee.

MICHAEL DUKAKIS is currently Governor of Massachusetts, a post he also held from 1974 through 1978. From 1978 through 1982 he was lecturer and director of intergovernmental studies at the John F. Kennedy School of Government. Areas of special interest include fiscal management reform and economic development policy at the federal, state, and local levels. Mr. Dukakis, along with Gordon Chase, was instrumental in creating Harvard's Program for Senior Executives in State and Local

Government, and in expanding the Kennedy School's involvement in state and local issues.

MARK H. MOORE is Daniel and Florence Guggenheim Professor of Criminal Justice Policy and Management at the John F. Kennedy School of Government. Drug abuse, gun control, and alcohol policies are among his current areas of research. His teaching emphasis is on the practical application of analytic techniques in public policy analysis. Professor Moore has served as special assistant to the administrator and director of the Office of Planning and Evaluation at the Drug Enforcement Agency.

RICHARD E. NEUSTADT is the Lucius N. Littauer Professor of Public Administration at Harvard University. Before coming to Harvard, Professor Neustadt taught at Columbia University and served on the Budget Bureau staff, on the White House staff under President Truman, and as a consultant to Presidents Johnson and Kennedy as well as to numerous federal executive and legislative bodies. His writings include *Presidential Power*, *Alliance Politics*, and, more recently, *The Swine Flu Affair* (with Harvey V. Fineberg).